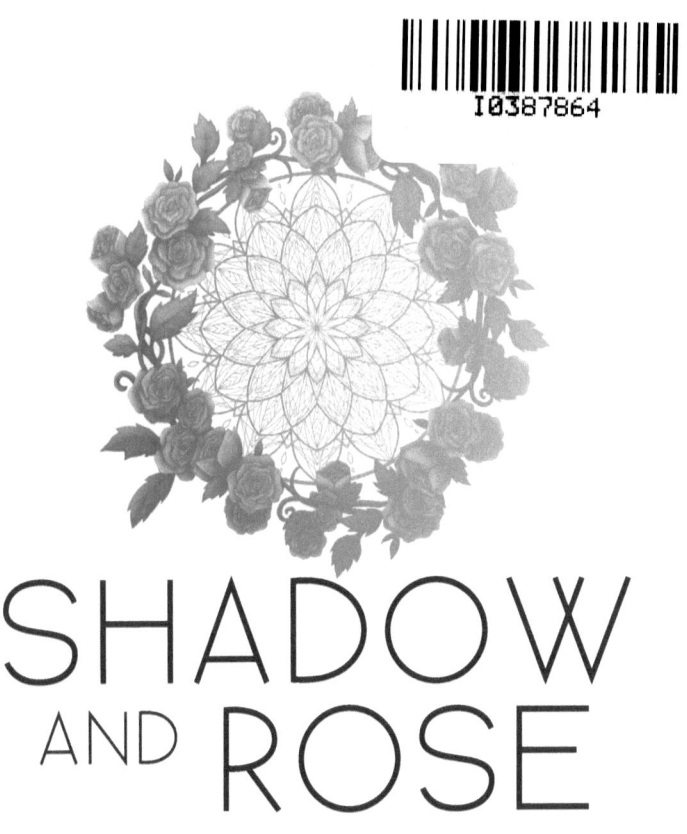

SHADOW AND ROSE

A SOULFUL GUIDE FOR WOMEN RECOVERING
FROM RAPE AND SEXUAL VIOLENCE

SHINE LIGHT ON YOUR HEART,
BLOOM INTO YOUR POWER.

SARAH WHEELER

Copyright © 2022 by Sarah Wheeler

All rights reserved. No part of this publication may be reproduced, distributed or transmitted in any form or by any means without permission of the publisher, except in the case of brief quotations referencing the body of work and in accordance with copyright law.

Cover Design by Kozakura @ fiverr.com/kozakura
Interior Design by Kozakura @ fiverr.com/kozakura

ISBN: 978-1-913590-58-1 (paperback)
ISBN: 978-1-913590-59-8 (ebook)

The Unbound Press
www.theunboundpress.com

SHADOW AND ROSE

SARAH WHEELER

For women everywhere;
recovering, retrieving, rising, thriving.

Shadow and Rose Online Resources at
www.youreenoughyoga.com
Password: **Recover2021**

Huge love and gratitude to my parents, partner, family, friends, mentors and teachers for your kindness and support while I worked on Shadow and Rose.

I also wish to thank my own Yoga teachers for their love, wisdom and expertise. Their emphasis on both empowering oneself and others, while also promoting critical thinking and autonomy have helped me feel empowered to craft this text and the accompanying meditations.

Hey unbound one!

Welcome to this magical book brought to you by The Unbound Press.

At The Unbound Press we believe that when women write freely from the fullest expression of who they are, it can't help but activate a feeling of deep connection and transformation in others. When we come together, we become more and we're changing the world, one book at a time!

This book has been carefully crafted by both the author and publisher with the intention of inspiring you to move ever more deeply into who you truly are.

We hope that this book helps you to connect with your Unbound Self and that you feel called to pass it on to others who want to live a more fully expressed life.

With much love,

Nicola Humber
Founder of The Unbound Press

PRAISE FOR SHADOW AND ROSE

A powerful book, woven through with the passion and conviction of a woman who knows what it is to rise above abuse and emerge more whole than ever before. Integrating and adapting, discovering hidden strengths and restoring the vital capacity to be open as a fully functioning woman – this book facilitates all of these things. It will support you, inspire you and keep you wonderful company on your journey through the healing territories.
— **Cathryn Deyn,** *Holistic Psychologist*

'Honest and heartfelt' is how I describe this book. Sarah has written a candid account of her experience of being sexually assaulted which is often seen as a taboo in society and the media. Sarah continues to explore societal attitudes and busts myths associated with sexual assault, all the while offering the reader a soothing insight into self-care and recovery. Sarah interweaves body-based techniques in supporting the reader to work through their trauma. The references to CBT (cognitive behavioural therapy), trauma presentations, yoga

and self-belief are important to Sarah who encapsulates an authentic and first-hand account of trauma.

I think anyone who has a suffered an interpersonal trauma will benefit from this book, as it is written from Sarah's perspective and not an 'expert in the field' who has not been traumatised. This makes the book feel more personable and relatable to the audience. The layout is broken down into parts; parts that often mirror the journey of someone who has been traumatised. The ending almost feels like a new beginning with reference to post-traumatic growth and healing.

I recommend this book to anyone who has an interest in Sarah's personal account of sexual assault, trauma and healing. The book is written in such a way that allows the audience to be captivated and bear witness to the complexities of interpersonal violence and trauma. Thank you Sarah for sharing your experiences in a thoughtful and insightful manner.

— **Practitioner Psychologist**,
Specialist in Trauma and Sexual Violence

CONTENTS

Praise For Shadow and Rose ix

Why We're Here 1

A Practical Note 9

What is Recovery? 13

What to Expect 17

Your Recovery Tools 21

WEEK ONE:
You have the Power: Recovering
Your Capacity to Heal 47

WEEK TWO:
You Did Not Deserve It and It Was Not
Your Fault-Recovering from Negative Self-Talk. 63

WEEK THREE:
More than just a Spa Day-Recovering Your
Right to Self-Care 77

WEEK FOUR:
Saying Yes to Yourself-Recovering Your
Boundaries and Voice 93

WEEK FIVE:
Letting Out Steam-Recovering
From Post-Traumatic Stress Disorder 109

WEEK SIX:
It Belongs in the Dark Ages-Recovering
from the Grip of Shame 137

WEEK SEVEN:
It is Right to be Raw-Recovering
Your Right to Sacred Rage 153

WEEK EIGHT:
Protecting the Inner Sanctum-Recovering the
Relationships You deserve 165

WEEK NINE:
Witching and Water-Recovering a
Connection to the Wild 177

WEEK TEN:
Woman, You're a Work of Art-Recovering Your
Connection with Your Body. 197

Finally, The F-Word: Forgiveness 225

Looking Forward 32

Resources for Recovery 235

Bibliography 239

Abbreviations 243

About the Author 245

chapter 1

WHY WE'RE HERE

Thank you for picking up this book. Thank you for reading these opening lines. I hope you stay now for a few more or come back another time. Every time you pick up this book, I want you to know that I've got your back.

I believe in you.

I believe you.

I hear you. I care about you. I care that you can grow to welcome your feelings, shine light on your pain and blossom into your power.

That might sound far-fetched because you are reading my words on a page and we don't know each other. Is it possible to really care about another human being without ever meeting them? I think it is, because when I was recovering from being sexually assaulted and raped, I wanted to connect with other survivors, other people on the journey to recovery. I wanted to show those who were struggling to recover (and I still struggle) that things slowly get better. I wanted to see living proof from other survivors, who were healing from their trauma, that life could be joyous again. Now, I am that living proof.

There's a cliché that everybody has a book in them, everybody has a story to tell. I always liked writing stories, essays and scripts. I didn't like writing poetry, but I was always willing to give it a shot. My English teachers often remarked that I had a nice flair for creative writing and that I could paint vivid pictures with words. Somewhere in the back of my mind was a thought that I could never shake off. I always knew I would write a book.

I liked the idea of writing a book, maybe a historical novel with inspiring female characters fighting to live their truth while under persecution by the Patriarchy, a Joan of Arc or a Wise Woman Witch. A story set hundreds of years ago, but relevant for modern readers. The kind of story, where you feel like you are reading about parts of your shadow through the characters. The parts of yourself that nobody sees, the parts of ourselves we attempt to disown, the many sides of ourselves that we barely even know, but that whisper to us in hushed tones.

I used to tell myself that, one day, I would sit and plan my novel, write down ideas having made a million mental notes of inspiration, order my thoughts, try to sketch out a plot and form characters. I have no idea how to write a novel. Instead, I got busy with other things.

Things that I really wanted to do like going to drama school, travelling, trying my luck in the acting business, being a teacher, working in a high-pressured sales job sat behind a desk for thirteen hours a day. I quit the last one on that list. Writing a story would have to wait until later. I told myself I would write when I had lots of time on my hands, I would write while on holidays, I would write when I felt inspired and only when I felt inspired, when I had earned enough money to be able to find time to do nothing but write (that hasn't happened!), or perhaps if I covertly slipped into the role of kept woman with sufficient side hustles, bringing in some income while a rich partner paid the bills. The whispers to write stayed in the shadows. Somehow, I couldn't find the truth that wanted to be expressed in the form of a novel.

I was never meant to write a novel. I was meant to write something else. The truth was to be told in another form. When we don't listen, the whispers grow louder, yet we ignore the voices that tell us to live our truth. This voice bumbling away in the recess of my mind got very loud and that is why I am tapping the keys on my laptop writing these words to you.

I'm writing this book to support your recovery from rape or sexual violence. I'm writing this book to let you know you have an ally in me. Rape Crisis England and Wales defines sexual violence as, 'Any unwanted sexual act or activity. There are many different kinds of sexual violence, including: rape, sexual abuse (including in childhood), sexual assault, sexual harassment, forced marriage, so-called honour-based violence, female genital mutilation (FGM), trafficking, sexual exploitation (including child sexual exploitation), and others.'

Sexual violence is an abhorrent, widespread crime. You have lived this kind of violence and you are very much not alone. The British Home Office states that roughly 11 adults in England and Wales are either raped or sexually assaulted by penetration every hour. In my opinion, this figure is just the tip of the iceberg because so many people choose not to report sexual violence to the police and, of those people who do report, only 1.7% of reported rape cases are prosecuted (The Home Office, 2019). The statistics for sexual violence around the world undoubtedly make for difficult reading.

On these pages you will find some guidance, ideas, tools, very gentle activities and relaxation techniques to help you with your recovery, but mostly you will find my love. Both gentle and fierce love. This was the book I was meant to write and you are meant to read this. People say writers should write about what they know. I know about recovering from being raped. I've lived it. I've lived the excruciating heartbreak, the numbness, the confusion, the raw rage of it, the trauma and stress, the pretending not to care, the projections of fear on to other people and the glimmers of changes in my life, which indicate that not only am I recovering, but that I am thriving. I know the path you are on and while our lives may look different, our journeys will share similarities.

As you recover, you are weaving your own narrative of the Heroine's Journey. You may have heard of the Hero's Journey that is a structure often used to form fiction, from novels to blockbuster films. It is a structure for narratives that has been widely consumed and popularised simply because the hero of the journey is a male. The world we live in favours the male and the masculine over the female and the feminine. This has been the case for thousands of years. Things are changing though and other stories are emerging. Stories that were woven thousands upon thousands of years ago at a time when the earth exalted feminine energy, while men and women lived in deeper union with the feminine energy of the Earth. For the most part, we have been privy to heroic masculine stories, which see the male hero setting out on a quest to prove his strength and valour, where he is challenged by obstacles like fire-breathing dragons and Bond villain-style baddies; but against the odds, he triumphs.

You are walking a journey that requires just as much resiliency, valour and strength. However, your story as a survivor is not about externally facing victories and prizes. Your Heroine's Journey and facing all its obstacles is taking a path toward retrieval. You will turn inward, not outward, to face your adversaries, which are the emotional and sometimes physical pains left over from being sexually violated. On the pages of this book, I reassure you that it is OK to be vulnerable, enraged and that keeping an open heart is possible as you retrieve the parts of yourself that rape attempted to steal. You will remember and recalibrate the essence of who you are. You are the Heroine in this journey. On this journey you are allowed every single one of your feelings and reactions while you heal. Imagine a Warrior Queen Creator-Destroyer Goddess Human standing next to you. That's me. I am here while you walk this path. You are that same Goddess. You have what it takes to look into the dark, into the flames that will sear away the old version of you and the pain, which you have been carrying, and to germinate the seeds of the new life into which you will bloom. The life you deserve.

You might feel all kinds of things at this point and you are allowed to feel all of it. Just because I've been raped too doesn't mean that I know exactly how you feel at this precise moment. I don't know what happened to you, but if you're reading this book out of choice or as recommended to you, I'm guessing you've been through some kind of sexual assault or rape/s. If nothing else, I want you to know that I'm writing this book with an enormous amount of love and it's all beaming toward you. Maybe that feels like too much? That's OK. You deserve every bit of love that wants to come your way. Love **will** come your way. I see you and I promise you that recovery is possible if you learn to care for yourself and let others support you too.

You might not agree with all the words. That is OK. Treat this book like buying clothes – try it on, see what fits and leave the rest. Some parts may seem like they were tailored especially for you.

Take everything in your recovery at your own pace. This is your life and you get to do with it whatever you please.

chapter 2

A PRACTICAL NOTE

I am a woman who was attacked by men in 21st century Patriarchal England. This is the context to my experience and my recovery. However, I truly hope my words can be of comfort to anyone from anywhere who has been sexually abused.

All sexual violence, no matter the gender of the survivor or perpetrator, is utterly deplorable and all perpetrators must be brought to justice. Sadly, we live within a system called Patriarchy, which still treats women, people of colour and those with disabilities as objects to be controlled predominantly by the white male. Patriarchal control plays out around the world attempting to inflict dominance over those who are not male and sexual violence is the brutal acting out of this dominance. This is a tough pill to swallow, yet please do not be disheartened. At the end of this book you will find resources, which offer practical support and guidance for recovery and seeking justice. Skip straight to that section now if needs be.

I began writing this book in April 2020, a year that changed so much for many people due to stay at home orders. Due to these orders, domestic abuse and violence against women increased. Calls to the National Domestic Abuse Helpline increased by 49% in the first three weeks of UK lockdown. The charity SafeLives states that 61% of domestic abuse survivors were not able to access online or in person support in 2020 because of monitoring by their perpetrator. The Office of National Statistics logged a rise in domestic violence in March to June 2020 compared with the same period in 2019, with a rise in domestic sexual offences since 2018 also being logged. Let's remember that these statistics only capture events **reported** and many women feel unable to report. The worldwide lockdowns which were planned supposedly for our safety, were arguably ineffective against Covid-19, yet still managed to wage war against women. This is a health crisis of its own. The work that needs to be carried out to protect women and bring their abuser to justice has been grossly underfunded by all governments. The Guardian journalists, Mary O'Hara and Katie Tarrant, reported in 2020 that £7,000,000 was cut from budgets that helped to support people recovering from domestic abuse between 2010 and 2018 due to austerity measures. The situation is now worse because already underfunded organisations are only able to offer remote services due to lockdown restrictions. At the time of completing this book the UK Domestic Abuse Bill had its second reading in Parliament and was due to become law in early 2021 offering hope to service users of domestic abuse charities which see many women being sexually abused at home. Please see the Resources section for support for recovering from domestic abuse.

This is a book to inspire healing and hope, for you to rise through recovery. Let me clearly state that this book and the relaxation techniques offered are not a substitute for professional clinical support for recovery from sexual violence or trauma. Please seek professional help if you are in distress or in danger. If you feel that taking the guided deep relaxation meditations, which accompany this text, is not for you at the moment, come back to them when you feel able. You are the one in control here and so if you do not feel good when trying the meditations or recovery rituals, stop the action and take care of yourself. Please be responsible for your own wellbeing.

chapter 3

WHAT IS RECOVERY?

This is the best way that I can sum up Recovery – Recovery is finding your way back to your Self. In life, things happen to us that can somehow make us forget who we are. Sexual violence is a prime example. Recovery is the process of removing the blockages (shame, fear, guilt, self-doubt, among others) that make us forget who we are. Nothing will take away the fact that you were attacked but you get to take your life back now. You deserve to be well and to thrive.

When I was raped, I had been in recovery from anorexia for about four years, so I was fortunate enough to have some experience with this process we call 'recovery.' I had already learned a few valuable lessons, which when I felt ready (and only when I felt ready) were able to help me to face recovery from sexual assault and rape. Let me reiterate: Your Recovery, Your Pace.

There are no quick fixes to recovery. It really is a process and yes, I know this sounds like one of those quotes that people bandy around in pretty typefaces on Instagram, but recovery is an ongoing journey, not a singular destination. Every day on your healing journey, you are coaxing out aspects of yourself that may have been hidden in the shadows. When we have enough compassion for ourselves to face our pain as survivors of sexual violence, there is the potential for magic to happen. This is the magic of you blossoming into your power, strengthened by what happened to you, not governed by the label of victimhood. Each one of us has the innate capacity for growth and healing. It is literally built into us, woven into our human fabric as an instinct; just like the instinct that leads glorious roses into bloom. You are a glorious rose. Yes, you are a glorious rose (insert the name of another flower here if you don't love roses). I promise you, you are a glorious flower, even on the days when you might feel like a piece of crap. I have those days too. Those days and feelings pass.

The journey of recovery can be a transformative one, if you let it. If you are willing to let your recovery be the vehicle for seeing aspects of yourself you may have once shied away from. If you are willing to let this path be a descent into your emotional wounds and a rising into your feminine power to recalibrate and retrieve the glorious pieces of yourself that perpetrators tried to erase. If you are willing to trust yourself, to let a little section of your heart stay open as you read this book and try the practices. If you are willing to consider that sexual violence is not the end, but an initiation into reclaiming your life and recovering.

chapter 4

WHAT TO EXPECT

Your Basic Tools

In this introductory chapter, I outline the main recovery tools, which I offer to you, week by week, as you progress through this book. You will be able to return to these tools time and time again. You may even develop your own lifelong practices inspired by the recovery journey, which you begin with this book.

Every week, read a chapter focused on a specific aspect of recovery. Each chapter includes an exercise to empower you in working with this piece of your recovery. Each chapter has a guided meditation recording for you, to help your mind and body relax into healing and to strengthen the work done in that week. These guided meditations are designed to elicit the body's 'Relaxation Response' so you may comfort and connect with yourself, while you rest your mind and body. You will find the recordings in the *Shadow and Rose* area on my website (www.youreenoughyoga.com). When you have finished reading each chapter, I encourage you to note down your progress for that week in your own journal.

chapter 5

YOUR RECOVERY TOOLS

You have the Power: Recovering Your Capacity to Heal

I have some very good news. Healing and recovery are states, which your body was designed for. In Week One, I introduce you to some basic knowledge about the design of your nervous system and how to consciously call on the biological wisdom of your nervous system for your recovery. This week, read about some of the ways in which people both inadvertently, understandably hinder the healing process. I empower you with some simple techniques, which you can use to help awaken your body's healing response, plugging into your own inbuilt healing system to create feelings of safety and calm.

You Didn't Deserve it and it Wasn't Your Fault. Recovering From Negative Self- Talk

Ever noticed that we, humans, are not very kind to ourselves? We talk about ourselves and to ourselves in ways in which we would never dream of talking to a friend. Unfortunately, this unkind self-talk often gets louder in the wake of painful life events. Through this week's words, I highlight the habit of negative self-talk and the pitfalls of continuing this habit while you are healing from sexual violence. I suggest a mantra you can use to comfort yourself when the negative mental chatter tries to get your attention. You will also choose a recovery mantra which suits you, that you can embed into this week's resting practice.

Not Just a Spa Day. Recovering Your Right to Sacred Self-Care

Having looked into the patterns of negative self-talk, you are on your way to developing a kinder relationship with yourself. As survivors, we deserve to give ourselves mega nurturing and kindness. Developing self-care habits is now essential. This week, you will read about what drives us to ignore sacred care, perhaps caring for others in place of caring for ourselves. It is time to lean in to look after your inner child. Planting the seeds for self-care this week prepares you for the journey of recovery.

Saying Yes to Yourself: Recovering Your Boundaries and Your Voice

This week, read what is meant by the term 'boundaries', what different types of boundaries there are and the possible damage to boundaries after sexual violence. You will discover the crucial skill of setting boundaries, which you can practise as part of your sacred self-care. In order to set boundaries, you need to have the willingness and courage to speak up for yourself. So this week, I guide you to reconnect with your voice, your autonomy and your right to set boundaries around what you wish to allow and not allow into your life. You will also hear from my very own therapist giving her view on boundaries as an act of self-love.

Letting Out Steam: Recovery from Post-Traumatic Stress Disorder (PTSD)

Many people are trying to get by in life while living with undiagnosed PTSD. Trauma is the body's response to events that were frightening, violent, violatory, shocking, unexpected and upsetting. Symptoms of trauma sometimes fade away on their own in a few weeks, but often trauma symptoms stick around for longer and make life and recovery more difficult. In this week's chapter, I tell you about my experience of living with PTSD and give you practical information about how to recognise the symptoms and how to access help if you think you may have PTSD, along with how to care for and honour yourself while you heal from trauma. I am delighted to be able to share an expert clinician's advice and insight on this topic. I also share with you the most valuable lessons I have learned, which help me live with and heal from trauma.

It Belongs in the Dark Ages: Recovering from the Grip of Shame

Shame is an insidious, coercive creature. I got to know shame intimately during my recovery. I came to know its script, body sensations and the false beliefs it tried to instil. From time to time, shame still makes an appearance in my life and I have got better at noticing it and sending it packing. Shame is something you do not need to live with, but if it does show up, shame can be a teacher. Shame does not belong to you. In this week's chapter, I give a feminine history lesson on the emergence of shame, how to recognise it and how to release it, so that you can live the life you deserve.

It's Right to Be Raw: Recovering Your Right to Rage

Have you ever felt like it was wrong/scary/bad manners/melodramatic to show your anger? Let alone to feel rage? Rage, fully acknowledged, welcomed and accepted, is powerful medicine, which alchemises into pure strength. This week, learn about a powerful, feminine emblem for rage and you may really want to be part of her gang after this week's reading and exercises. You have the right to be angry. Women have a lot to be angry about, especially those of you who are reading this book. This week, explore how anger can be a catalyst for change, rather than a state to be stuck and suffer in.

Protecting the Inner Sanctum: Recovering the Relationships You Deserve

While you are recovering from sexual violence, you are at your most vulnerable to the game-playing of toxic people. There will be some people to whom your recovery is something of a threat because you are re-learning autonomy and wresting the driving seat of your life back into your own hands. I can vouch for this because it has happened to me. I am an empath and I have had an energetic pattern of unconsciously attracting people into my life who are not good for me; therefore they are toxic to my health. I used to give people far too many chances when they treated me badly. This is because I am an empath and had a deep-rooted tendency for rescuing others, (even though I should have been using my energy to recover and rescue myself). However, it is also due to the fact that as women, we are encouraged to always be nurturing and caring to people, even if some are unhealthy for us. In this week's chapter, I point out some of the feelings you may be experiencing if you have been in toxic relationships and the 'red flag' behaviours of toxic people so you can spot them early and, through the support of a therapist, learn to ring-fence your recovery.

Witching and Water: Recovering Your Connection with the Wild

You don't have to be a hippy like me to appreciate and soak up the Earth's bounty as part of your recovery process. In this week's chapter, I share with you my joy of being outdoors and connecting with nature. Nature is here for you, offering many sacred tonics and elixirs, whether this be a blustery walk in your nearest park, potting herbs on your kitchen windowsill or immersing yourself in healing waters while wild swimming. You see, inside you, lives a wise, wild woman who needs to be fed by the natural world. Perhaps, your healing journey will coax her forward, untethered, to be your ally for the rest of your life.

Woman You're a Work of Art: Recovering Your Relationship with Your Body

This week, read about and ponder regaining your connection with your physical body. Our bodies are there for us and take much grief from the wear and tear of our feet. Our spine is literally holding us up to the burden the body must bear while it tries to recalibrate from the shock of sexual violence. In this week's chapter, I share with you my journey to something akin to body acceptance while I invite you to consider all the ways your body works for you and not against you. I intend that over time you can accept and enjoy the skin you are in while taking care of your physical health.

My Heartfelt Rosey Intention

I intend that having read this book, week by week, and having taken part in the guided relaxations, you will have grown in self-compassion, you will be honing your body's intrinsic capability to relax and heal itself while unfurling into your personal power and strength. You have the right to recover and the right to thrive.

Tools to Help You Heal

- ### Healing Tool: Yoga Nidrā

You may never have heard of yoga nidrā, or perhaps you are familiar with this term, if you practise Yoga. Since the 20th century, yoga nidrā has been widely 'understood to be a guided meditation technique' (Birch and Hargreaves, 2015) with a specific set of steps always practised in a supine position. Contrary to what you may already know, yoga nidrā is not singularly a technique or yoga posture. Yoga nidrā is an altered state of consciousness similar to sleep, but which is beyond the three regular states of sleep, dreaming and wakefulness. This altered state may be experienced at any point during guided deep relaxation when we practise drawing our attention away from external stimuli.

This altered state is named after the Goddess Yoganidrā in a text called the *Devi Mahatmya* dating back to 300BCE–300CE in which the Goddess manifests as sleep. The state or possibility of yoga nidrā was written about and practised hundreds of years before the disgraced teacher/guru Swami Satyananda created his set of rigid, specific instructions and scripts for what became known as the formalised technique of 'Satyananda Yoga Nidrā.' This set of instructions, methodology and scripts were later trademarked by the Bihar School of Yoga. I heard a 'Satyananda Yoga Nidrā' script once and did not connect with it, and so chose to listen to different types of yoga nidrā practices. Following Gurus like Satyananda has never sat well with me and I do not teach 'Satyananda Yoga Nidrā'. I was trained in 'Empowered Wisdom Yoga Nidrā. For me, yoga nidrā goes beyond a technique prescribed by a single teacher, owned by a yoga institute because yoga nidrā did not begin this way. Yoga nidrā is not singularly a methodology, something to do, eventually packaged by Satyananda but is a state to be experienced and embodied over time.

Deep relaxation to drop into the state of yoga nidrā is one of the key tools, which has aided my recovery, not only from sexual violence, but also from addiction, exhaustion and Anorexia. Yoga nidrā has helped me to feel calmer, softer and way less defensive. It is this deep state of relaxation beyond the usual states of sleep, waking and dreaming, which I refer to in this book as yoga nidrā. This soothing, nourishing state has become part of my life and my recovery. Yoga in the ancient language of Sanskrit means union or yoking of individual to the collective and union between body, mind and spirit. 'Ni' means void and 'drā' means draw forth. So in the state of yoga nidrā we experience union with the void that is brought forward. In the guided relaxation practices, which accompany this book, you will practise bringing your body, mind and consciousness into union through cultivating a deeply relaxed state, which brings forth a liminal space in which the body and mind can sleep, while your consciousness remains aware. This is the void. Your awareness will rest in the safety of the void. Remember that should you choose to take these guided relaxations, practise at your own pace and for as short or as long as you see fit. You are in charge.

Yoga nidrā is extremely beneficial for calming an anxious body and mind. If you have never stepped onto a yoga mat in your life or you have not tried any type of yoga before, that literally does not matter because these guided relaxations can be experienced while sitting (even on a chair) or lying in a position in which you feel very comfortable.[1] You need to take time at the start of your practice to ensure you are feeling totally comfortable in your body positioning. For more guidance on setting up the area for your yoga nidrā, be sure to watch the video on nest-building in the *Shadow and Rose* area on my website (www.youreenoughyoga.com). Some yoga nidrā teachers say you must stay in one position for the whole duration of the session, which is usually about 30 minutes, but I say go ahead and adjust your position if you wish to. The beauty of yoga nidrā is that you can do this practice at home, or at a friend's home if you need to be somewhere away from your own home to get some peace and to guarantee not being disturbed.

In a nutshell (or rosebud) this is what happens in a yoga nidrā session:

You sit cross-legged, supported by a wall, or lie down on your back (whichever feels more appropriate for you at this stage) and do yourself the kindness of getting very comfortable in a nest made from some pillows and blankets, which you can gather from around your home.

---

[1] I want to address the fact that NOBODY needs to be good at/experienced/fit or spiritual to reap the benefits of yoga. There are various types of yoga and, over time, people find the right style that suits them best. I teach Hatha Yoga and yoga nidrā, with a bit of Vinyasa Yoga and Restorative Yoga too. Hatha classes have more stillness in the physical shapes than Vinyasa classes, which are quicker in pace and have more flowing movements. Restorative Yoga incorporates different shapes in which the body tissues can relax and involves lots of getting comfortable and supported with blankets and pillows. Yoga nidrā is practised in stillness and is a beautiful way to start to learn to feel safe, calm and self-compassionate while appearing to be doing nothing.

The teacher guides you through a gentle breathing exercise and may invite you to mentally set a resolve (a strong intention) for your session. You do not have to close your eyes if you do not wish to.

You listen to the teacher instructing you to let your mind notice your breath or parts of your body. They might suggest that you visualise an image or symbol too such as a moon or a setting where you have felt safe and content.

You are reminded to let your physical body fall asleep along with your mind, while your awareness stays awake hearing the instructions.

The session ends after about 20 to 30 minutes.

One style of deep relaxation for guiding us toward yoga nidrā sees us allowing our bodies to fully relax, bit by bit. Some styles of guided deep relaxation practice see the practitioner (you) directing your consciousness around your body parts with the intention of allowing your body to relax. By relaxing your body you will also rest your mind without *trying* to focus or concentrate on relaxing your mind.

Have you ever been told to clear, empty or relax your mind? Usually, it does not work because while we are going about our daily lives, our brains have way too much stuff to think about to even have space to relax. In this typical waking state, the mind cannot actually experience relaxation, but will end up thinking about a memory of relaxation or perhaps analysing why relaxation seems impossible, rather than having a chance to dip below its busy state into a place of genuine stillness. When you train your mind and body with relaxation techniques and time in the state of yoga nidrā, the more you will be able to guide yourself into relaxation as you listen to the teacher's yoga nidrā instructions. In time, you may choose to self-guide and no longer listen to recorded yoga nidrā, or not; the choice for how you practise is yours. Our body, mind and spirit can only heal when we have the chance to enter a less frazzled state than the one in which humans typically live. When people are feeling frazzled or overwhelmed by being busy, brainwaves are short and frequent. If we want to induce deep relaxation, we need to give the brain a chance to produce longer, less frequent waves. To give the brain an opportunity to produce these longer brainwaves, we need to reduce the stimuli which the brain is given, thereby reducing the amount of external information for it to process. The ancient sage, Patanjali, stated that 'Pratyahara', meaning withdrawing the senses from external stimuli, is one of the pathways to Yoga (union).

Humans are overstimulated creatures. I certainly used to overstimulate my brain and definitely had a tendency to pressure myself to cram lots into my days, all while keeping an eye on my emails and trying to resist the temptation of quick gratification on social media. However, my tendency towards anxiety spiked after I was sexually assaulted and so my brain was in overdrive, scanning constantly for danger and frenziedly trying to problem-solve. If I had kept myself as busy as I used to be, I would not have allowed myself the chance to slow down and access the deep relaxation, which my body craved. You may have responsibilities to other people that keep you busy such as a busy job and/or children and it can be hard to take time for oneself if this is the case. While you recover you may want to ask a trusted friend or colleague for support with some of your responsibilities so that you can have some space for tending to your healing.

Our bodies want to heal, but we must gift them the right conditions. These conditions are conscious rest, body relaxation and replenishing our energy reserves. I am asserting that deep relaxation for accessing yoga nidrā is an accessible and practical self-care tool that all of us can practise to empower ourselves to be healers in our own recovery. As a yoga teacher and Reiki Master, the above conditions are the practices which I care most about and gently encourage students and clients to weave into their daily lives. When I chose to learn more about the link between healing and relaxation, I often referred to a brilliant scientific text called *The Relaxation Response*. I mention it a few times in this book for sure! In this text, medical doctor, Herbert Benson, and Miriam Z. Klipper expand on the notion that we must consciously create the right conditions for our bodies to be able to take proper relaxation, as opposed to thinking we are relaxing by doing distraction activities such as compulsively watching re-runs of comedies on Netflix, whilst scrolling through Instagram (I have definitely done these things!). In the next chapter, I explain more about these right conditions for relaxation.

Rest is not a luxury but a priority and, while you recover from the things that happened to you, it is crucial. Rest is a state which our body needs. In fact, rest is so crucial that I recommend you continue to weave resting practices into your life for long after you have finished reading this book! There are pre-recorded deep relaxation meditations for experiencing the graceful state of yoga nidrā in the *Shadow and Rose* area on my website (www.youreenoughyoga.com). I invite you to use these recordings as a program to begin your long-term recovery. I recommend that you allow yourself the time and space to do these guided relaxations at least five times a week.

I know that it can feel challenging to be still after a trauma like sexual violence. Do remember that YOU oversee how to try the deep relaxation exercises for experiencing yoga nidrā, so if stillness for the whole session feels too much right now, you can leave the guided practices until you feel more ready to consider being still. Remember that you are free to shift position at any time in the deep relaxations which I provide.

Typically, when people think about yoga classes, they envisage a group of people, each on their own yoga mat, making various poses or shapes guided by a teacher. This is an accurate perception of a yoga class because typically yoga classes focus on the physical aspect of yoga, which in

Sanskrit is called 'asana.' However, yoga has seven other 'limbs' or aspects, which include meditation, concentration, withdrawal of the senses, along with suggested ways of behaving, which encourage us to be kind to ourselves and others. You do not need to be strong or flexible or fit or co-ordinated to try the physical aspect of yoga (asana). I suggest to people who attend my yoga classes that these are the bonus prizes of a physical yoga practice. Trying yoga asanas in a class taught by a teacher, whom you feel comfortable with, is another lovely way to be kind to your body while you are recovering.

Post Script on Yoga Nidrā: Guru Abuse

It is crucial for me to be transparent and state that Swami Satyananda was accused of sexual abuse in 2014. He caused harm to many people and I stand with and send love to the people he traumatised. I found out about the abuse while writing this book and feel it is crucial for me as a yoga teacher to address this abhorrence, most importantly because of the subject of this book. I was utterly sickened and angered to learn that Satyananda who has become synonymous with the trademarked technique/methodology he dubbed 'Satyanada Yoga Nidrā,' was exposed as an abuser. I was livid to read about his crimes and felt conflicted about standing by the practice of deep relaxation to evoke the presence of Goddess Yoganidrā. He is just one on a list of male yoga teachers including K. Pattabhi Jois (purported founder of Ashtanga Yoga),

Swami Vishnudevananda (Sivananda Yoga), Yogi Bhajan (founder of Kundalini Yoga and the face of Yogi Tea) and Bikram Choudhury (founder of Bikram Yoga) who have abused power over yoga students for their own gain in cultic organisations. I initially encountered the practice of deep relaxation and the experience of the state of yoga nidrā while I was recovering from sexual violence, never in connection with Bihar or Satyananda. In this case I feel it is possible to engage in deep relaxation and to witness the altered state named after Goddess Yoganidrā without being bound by Satyananda's modernised instructions or his version of the practice, hence my choice to continue to engage with yoga nidrā as a healing practice and I stand by its validity for eliciting relaxation and the healing response from deep rest.

Satyananda's method is not what I am teaching and not what I was taught. Indeed, techniques for entering this altered state of deep relaxation and awareness have been practised for centuries as explained in several ancient Hatha Yoga and Raja Yoga texts such as The Yoga Sutras of Patanjali and Hathayogapradipika. The deep relaxation, from which the state of yoga nidrā can arise has been engaged with as a meditational technique perhaps even further back than 12th century Laya Yoga practices. As a yoga teacher it is this combination of Laya Yoga meditational and relaxational practices, along with reverence for the Goddess Yoganidrā which inform my own teaching and practice rather than any adherence to Satyananda. I would never suggest that Satyanada's victims continue to practice his methodology and I hope his victims are given reparations and the help to recover. As a way to boycott Satyananda I will not be purchasing any books from the guru affiliated Yoga Publications Trust or engaging in any Satyananda methodology. It is not OK for teachers or yoga studios to promote the work or methodology of an abuser. I will continue to be transparent about the violence of this guru who is so unfortunately linked to yogic relaxation techniques and erroneously associated with separate yoga nidrā practices.

- ## Rest and Relaxation are Your Birth Right

Humans have at best, an on-off relationship with rest. About 10 years ago, rest and I were mainly off. If you are anything like me, you might have grown up believing the myth that rest is a luxury. Did you ever hear anything like this? *You can relax/ watch TV/ play/ do colouring/ sleep when you've done your homework, tidied your room, cleaned out the hamster and helped with dinner.* There is nothing wrong with carers wanting young ones to help around the home, in fact it is such a vital tool to train young people to have some idea of how to look after themselves in later life. In truth, I barely had any chores to do and I am still rather inept at housework aged 35. What I'm illustrating here is that we take cues from other people's behaviour, usually our parents. And what we see, we can end up doing and believing. We usually don't question a behaviour or belief until our lives require us to do so.

When I was growing up, nobody demonstrated for me the importance of relaxation and rest as life skills.

I worked in sales for a couple of years. I had several types of to-do lists, yes several, because there was so much to do and handle in my job that the probability of completing all items on any list was slim to none. Every time somebody requested a piece of work, a meeting needing to be scheduled, a report written, a target plan for the next quarter, a complaint to resolve, a piece of homework (yes in this job we had homework from staff training calls each week), even taking clothes to the dry cleaner, renewing my travel pass, leisure activities, going to a yoga class – everything had to go on the lists. The list, which a task was recorded on, depended on the task's urgency. In this workplace productivity was God. Missing my daily target for sales was not an option and not acceptable. I was literally told this in my early days in the role. The culture of the work environment was one of meet your sales targets, no matter what. If this meant not leaving your desk in the sales department for hours and taking 20 minutes to eat lunch while dialling the phone at the same time, so be it. Rest did not feel important or urgent while I was being watched for my productivity each day. Rest activities such as going for a yoga or meditation class or having a massage were always shoved into my to-do list of items that I would get to another time, not this week, but some day.

Failing to prioritise rest is a disaster waiting to happen. We live in a culture in which being rushed off our feet and living off fumes is a bizarre badge of honour. People get sick because we do not rest our body and mind. I used to think that this busy-ness just applied to women, but it's everybody. Adults, teenagers and children can end up all so busy. We are indoctrinated from a very young age to be busy (go to drama club, learn an instrument, ballet lessons, sports, art club, 6am swim training and that's on top of school and homework), and while young people often have a lot of energy and want constant stimulation, it doesn't mean it's healthy to schedule our children and ourselves into full activity calendar oblivion. Even though you may describe yourself as busy, what is your busy-ness actually accomplishing that allows you to feel at peace and nourished? Being overly busy can be an unfulfilled cycle and unfulfilling lifestyle.

The incredible, holistic system, which our body, mind and spirit form, requires rest, not just squeezing in six hours of sleep each night, but incorporating additional daily intervals to simply sit or lie down in relaxation. Does this sound unachievable for you or out of your comfort zone? It was out of mine as well, until I quit my sales job because my body had manifested terrible migraines, in which I would get paralysis down one side, dizzying nausea, slurred speech and untold pain. The neurologist, who treated me for over a year, was confident that I would get better but I would need preventative medication for a very long while. But something had to change that medication would not cure, and that was my living-on-fumes, exhausting lifestyle. To cut a longer story short, I had to learn to rest and relax.

I learned to rest and relax because my health depended on it. I am able to write to you as a result of having made space in my life for rest. Relaxation practices like meditation and the altered state of yoga nidrā not only catalyse healing across the physical, mental, emotional and spiritual planes but also allow for the literal headspace for creativity to find its way. For our voice and ideas to make themselves heard, we need to give them room to surface and breathe. Your recovery also needs room to breathe and blossom.

· Healing Tool: Free writing

Free writing does not need a whole bunch of explanation. You do not have to be a good writer or in any way creative to use this healing tool and to benefit from it. After every guided yoga nidrā, I invite you to free write for between five and 10 minutes. You are welcome to write for longer if your pen seems to want to. Essentially, free writing is writing down freely whatever has come to mind or into your heart after a period of meditation or a ritual. It is different from journaling because there is no specific theme to write about and no question to answer. It is simply writing down whatever is present for you after an exercise. You needn't read over your notes or try to analyse where your words came from after you have finished writing, as much less attention need be given to what your musings mean. However, I do suggest that you free write on to paper though rather than typing on to a device after deep relaxation.

- Healing Tool: Acknowledge Your Progress

This is another very simple writing practice to complete at the end of each week. At the close of each chapter, note down at least two things from the week, or weeks if you are taking each chapter at a slower pace, that you feel mark progress you have made during that time. Honestly, it could be the most mundane things. For example, your turning down an invite to go out when you really needed to stay home or you took 20 minutes of You-Time to have a walk outside. You might notice that after a couple of weeks you are putting together a trove of notes about things you feel proud of and actions that have supported your budding self-care.

- Healing Tool: Roses

> *'The Roses, the Roses, it was the bloody Roses'*
> **– Robert Hunter, Lyricist**

There's no other way to say this, other than I am crazy about roses. I'm almost obsessed about these stunning creations that we are lucky enough to be able to spot without searching too hard. I have always adored roses and as a child I was content for hours in my parents' back garden making a very classy concoction called rose water perfume. This consisted of rose petals and water mixed around with a paintbrush in a jam jar. I would leave this potion for a day or so to do its magic. I would come back to my creation and breathe in the heavenly scent, which laced the water. I liked nothing more than to dab it on my wrists and my neck, adorning myself with the wet petals too. Then I grew up and stopped making rose water perfume, but I kept that memory close. I would remember Child Sarah making her rose magic whenever I picked up the scent of roses.

After the first time I was sexually assaulted, I started having therapy at the wonderful Havens centre in London. For their contact details, see the link on my Resources page at the back of this book. My therapist mentioned that I could try doing small kindnesses to myself. I had resisted this self-care business for a long time, right up until that moment when there I was being desperate enough to try anything to help myself in the aftermath of the attack. Roses immediately sprang to mind. I walked into the Tesco in Whitechapel and bought myself a small bunch of pale pink roses. As tears welled up, I stared into the endless swirls inside the blooms. I saw the beauty and I felt hope. These precious flowers were saving me. Since that day, everywhere I turned there were roses and they silently whispered, 'Heal with us.'

Roses grow in parks, rising up through the soil in public flowerbeds. You can see them tied with stems chopped in bunches in supermarkets. They may catch your eye over the wall in someone's garden or window box, or perhaps you are fortunate to have some of your own blossoming for you. Before roses found their way to your local shops, they travelled from afar and have stood the test of time with rose fossils dating back at least 35 million years to ancient Persia. This is certainly magical staying power as roses have been around way longer than humans with the fossil record showing our ancient ancestors showing up around two million years ago. Very early civilisations, including the Egyptians and the Chinese, grew roses purely for pleasure so they could drink in their beauty and also use the petals to make rose oil for anointing rituals. Roses have long been associated with femininity, secrets, beauty and healing. It's written in the myths that red roses come from the Greek Goddess of Love, Aphrodite's blood dripping on to a pure white rose as she ran over thorns to reach her lover.

Roses have held a special place in the human psyche for millennia, their swirling pattern an imprint of the swirling geometry of the cosmos. Some researchers draw a comparison between the rose in Western tradition with the lotus flower in Eastern tradition. Both of these flowers are symbolic of human consciousness, our ability to drop roots into the earth and rise up through the muddy ground or murky waters overcoming obstacles that could hinder our growth on the way. I think this is why roses light me up so much because they are a true symbol for healing, growing into our power and having the courage to do so when the odds are against us. Roses are a symbol of resistance against Patriarchy. They have a transformational impact and literally alter how we feel through our senses. We are drawn out of the oppressive systems and can surrender into their gentle power. You have this delicate power inside of you too. Your highest self, the roses and I have got your back.

In each week's reading or exercises you will find something rose-related to add some beauty into your recovery journey. For me, roses are the perfect symbol for returning to yourself as you experience so many layers of healing, the soft petals unfolding as you unfold to recover yourself.

I scatter rose petals at the feet of every woman who reads this book.

chapter 6

WEEK ONE:

YOU HAVE THE POWER: RECOVERING YOUR CAPACITY TO HEAL

This first week is about allowing our bodies to relax so that our natural capacity for self-healing can flower. When we relax fully, which you will practise doing over time, your body and mind can let go of being vigilant and, instead can receive the nourishment of relaxation. Our bodies are amazing, we literally have an inbuilt system called the Autonomic Nervous System (ANS) which is designed to help us survive danger when threatened, while enabling growth, repair and flourishing when at rest. The part of the ANS, which promotes feelings of wellbeing and repair, is called the Parasympathetic Nervous

> System (PNS). However, every human being needs balance and so we have another system called the Sympathetic Nervous System (SNS).

The SNS is like the high-functioning twin of the PNS. The SNS gets triggered when we need to be alert to danger, but the SNS can become overactive and keep us feeling overly stimulated a lot of the time. This can lead to stress, exhaustion and 'burn out,' but in the stress cycle it feels like the chicken and egg situation; what is coming first? Is it stress or activation of the SNS sending you into the response popularly termed 'fight or flight' or the more primal freeze state? A body system in permanent stress cannot easily access the healing state because the SNS is simply too active; making relaxation seem out of reach. For relaxation and healing to occur we must practise down-regulating the SNS. In this chapter, I outline some of the science of relaxation and how it generates the human body's inbuilt chill-out healing response. This week's occasion of deep relaxation will help you to feel grounded while enabling you to experience the right conditions for eliciting deep relaxation.

Let me tell you a bit more about me, as some context for your own path into healing. I grew up in Gloucestershire. I live in Brighton. I love swimming in the sea, hummus is my favourite food, and roses are my favourite flower. I love peanut M&Ms and it's a shame they don't make vegan ones. I'm an entrepreneur. I am an artist, women's workshop facilitator, yoga teacher, founder of the brand, *You're Enough Yoga*, and I am a Reiki Teacher .

I care about living in a world where everybody feels they are enough just as they are. I'm on a Warrior-Queen mission to bust the myths and heal the wounds of being 'not enough' or 'too much'. Yoga, Reiki and art are some of the tools in my apothecary for healing these wounds that have been inflicted by the Patriarchy. That's my life these days, but a few years ago, things were very different.

In July 2016, I was sexually assaulted and diagnosed with PTSD as a result of this attack. In March 2017, I was raped twice. These were terrible experiences, and for sure, I wish these events had not happened. However, having lived these experiences and being in ongoing recovery, I am clear that these events have shaped who I am for the better. Naturally, in the immediate aftermath, I felt that my world was falling apart and my heart broke into even deeper crevices with each attack. It's a paradox because I am thriving in recovery and, of course, wish I had never been attacked.

Things were tough for a couple of years. These crimes committed against me were the most cataclysmically terrible experiences of my life. I had PTSD, relapsed into self-harm, a brief eating disorder relapse and severe reactive depression. I tried suicide a couple of times. I'm glad my attempts failed, but at the time, I promise you

I wanted to get the hell off this planet and just melt into the arms of the Universe. I am still recovering from the attacks but I now know myself as a vividly alive, vibrant, attractive and desirable woman. I'm not going to feed you any notion that healing from rape is easy, time efficient or logical. There is no paint-by-numbers-process for recovery; there are no quick fixes. I also want you to know that I am not your healer. You, my love, are your healer. The tools and musings in this book are here as a catalyst and rose-infused backdrop to your own capacity to elicit change and healing as you move forward on your journey.

Willingness is key though. Perhaps I should have listed 'being willing' as one of the recovery tools! You are the Mistress of your inner and outer world and so you already have the power to soothe yourself toward wellness. And I do understand if you feel the opposite of powerful right now. Being willing to care enough about yourself to fully lean right into your recovery may sound like an obvious thing to highlight; if you didn't want to recover and move forward, then you wouldn't be reading this book, right? However, our minds can be tricky creatures laced up tight into old patterns of behaviour and habits that can thwart us on the road to recovery. For example, when I chose that my life would no longer be about anorexia, starving myself of food and love. I acknowledged – with the help of a counsellor – that being ill and sad actually had a couple of payoffs and I would need to give these up. Being sad all the time, self-destructive and physically weak brought me a lot of attention from people who loved me. Of course, they were willing to give me this attention, but I used their attention as a creepy kind of validation instead of, little by little, finding the courage to let go of the Sick Sarah and become a Healthy Sarah. *What if people didn't like me as much as when I was ill? What if I would have to get strong enough to be able to care about myself instead of relying on others to do it for me?* These questions unsettled me but I chose to be willing to get well. Day by day, I practised being willing to choose life over the death jaws of an eating disorder. This experience of recovering from anorexia supported me after I was sexually assaulted in 2016. Take some time to consider what thought patterns, behaviours or beliefs may challenge your willingness to recover. You may like to look at the therapy resources at the end of the book for support with this.

Creating the conditions for healing is our own responsibility (and I do understand that the levels of socio-economic privilege we are born with can be a help or hinderance when creating the conditions for recovery). We must not only rely on others to create the healing conditions for us, although many people will want to help you, which can be supportive. Years ago, lots of people wanted me to recover from anorexia and offered their help on many occasions which I am eternally grateful for. A very scared, childlike part of me clung to that eating disorder like a stubborn limpet on a rock, because it was a familiar behaviour pattern, but also very much like the toxic best friend who wants to steal your partner. Anorexia wants to steal life. There was a missing piece amongst all this help though, and that was me. I had not said yes to my own recovery. Receiving help is awesome and can be a courageous act in itself for the fiercely independent I-don't-need-you types out there. However, we have to be WILLING to receive our own help to bring ourselves back into enough alignment with life itself so that body, mind and spirit can settle into the healing state. It can be a relief to remember, when we say yes to ourselves, when we care enough about ourselves to step on to the path to recovery after sexual violence, that we have taken what I think is the biggest step on the journey.

There will be bad days where things might feel horrendous, where you may do unhelpful/unkind behaviours toward yourself like drinking too much wine (spirits were my go-to), take too many drugs, over-exercise, undereat/overeat or fall into a spiral of negative self-talk. We all have different ways of coping. Please do not judge yourself harshly for doing stuff like this while you are recovering.

Recovery is totally possible. At the precipice of stepping on to your journey to recover who you are, I want you to know that it is all possible and if you are dreaming of feeling a lot better than how you have been feeling; you **can** heal. That being said, recovery and healing are the most inconvenient of journeys. Trauma has no interest in the rational or fathomable. Things often felt like one step forward and two steps back. I saw a postcard once with the caption 'Healing Is Not Linear.' I was annoyed by the phrase, but it somehow resonated so I bought it to remind me.

To my annoyance, the quote on the postcard turned out to be correct. Years since buying that postcard from a shop in a London station, my irritation has morphed into relief and I see that postcard every day on my nature altar, reminding me that where I am is OK and I can choose recovery in any moment, even if I have been having a shitty day. Healing isn't something that is goal-based that we need to sit and focus on, but healing is both a physiological and psychological response, a continuous state that our bodies can produce if we create the optimum conditions. There will be bumps in the road on our healing journey, things like fear and anxiety, which may get triggered, but this is to be expected. I like to view things like fear, stress and anxiety not as obstacles, which block recovery, but as part of the journey **to** recovery. It may be helpful to consider that recovery from sexual violence is not about getting over something and swiftly moving on, but instead it is learning to live with what happened while remembering that you deserve a good life.

We all have to start somewhere when recovering from sexual violence and, you, my love, might have found this book at any stage of recovery; maybe you were attacked very recently, or a number of months or years ago. Wherever you are IS wherever you are. I'm sure that you would rather not be in the situation of suffering whatever sexually violent situation you found yourself in. You may feel resentful or straight up angry that you need to be reading this book because, let's be real, given the choice you would rather not have been attacked. I wish I had not been sexually assaulted and raped and harassed. But I was. You and I are just normal people trying to do the best we can in our lives whilst also being courageous enough to navigate the ups and downs of the healing process. I hope you can give yourself compassion, not just because self-compassion is literally physically healthy for you, but also so you can rest assured that you are where you are, that it's OK and you will get better.

I am a Reiki Master so I like to talk about things like healing, energy and finding our true selves. I like to think of healing as waking up to our sense of wholeness. External factors throughout life sometimes lead us to believe that we are broken, not good enough or even 'damaged goods,' which is a particularly vile, objectifying and untrue epithet. This could be anything from our parents getting divorced when we were very young, being bullied at school or at work when we were older. Acts of sexual violence are the kind of external factors that can definitely lead us to believe that we are defective, damaged goods. The events that happen to us do not mean anything about us. Being sexually abused, assaulted or raped means nothing about you, much less that you are anything like broken. You might *feel* broken, that is understandable, but our feelings are not the whole truth, more like an indicator of the harm done to us. Your whole truth is that you are whole as you are, with nothing added or taken away.

Here Comes the Scientific Bit

When we are unable to relax, it is often due to our body and mind being triggered too frequently into a state which, way back in 1915, scientist, Walter Cannon, dubbed 'fight or flight;' also known as hyperarousal. This state can be triggered in the SNS when the ANS instinctively senses danger and directs the SNS to react, so one can change their behaviour by escaping or fight back when trying to save themselves from a genuine or perceived threat. When the SNS is alerted, the body's energy gets sent direct to the limbs rather than to the central organs so that one can move fast or react to defend themselves. This is a helpful response triggered in the body when a genuine danger occurs and we need to get away.

For some people (like me, when I was attacked) when faced with a threat perceived as life- threatening, trying to move the body to escape the danger simply doesn't work and they freeze. The freeze state is called hypoarousal. Freezing is the human body's most primal defence reaction, in effect playing-dead to save itself. The freeze response is the nervous system's oldest response to danger and has stayed with us through human evolution. When in the freeze state, people may feel completely disconnected from their body, unable to feel because they have become numb as the pain threshold rises to save us from the physical pain of an attack. The freeze response is deployed by the ANS only when the nervous system senses the most serious life-threatening dangers so that an organism can attempt to save its own life. The freeze response is likely to be instinctively deployed during an instance of sexual violence.

When faced with danger, we legitimately do need to react to try to protect ourselves, whether this be self-defence, fleeing or, like a frightened animal, freezing. However, after surviving frightening attacks such as sexual violence, some people find themselves far more jumpy, anxious and easily unnerved in so-called normal situations where no threat or danger is occurring. Some argue that the body and mind can get caught in perpetual arousal of the SNS in which a specific set of physiological responses happen. In this kind of frightened arousal, the heart rate speeds up, breathing becomes more rapid, oxygenated blood rushes away from organs of the digestive system and out toward the limbs to prepare to fight or run away, while a mental state of anxiety may linger as the brain scans for more danger. If you are faced with an overactive SNS, the body is likely to become drained of energy and very fatigued, along with a host of other physical symptoms which you will read more about in the chapter about PTSD. Too much stress (felt when the hormones cortisol, adrenaline and norepinephrine release), anxiety and fear swing the body out of its natural state of balance and far away from rest, repair and the state of calm, which is the domain of the PNS.

In the 1970s, Dr. Herbert Benson suggested and proved in his Harvard University studies that the more time a person spends feeling mentally and physiologically relaxed with the PNS more dominant than its more highly-strung twin, the SNS, the greater their chances of recovering from the effects of high blood pressure (hypertension). High blood pressure relates to anxiety and stress, which is massively contributed to by the fight or flight response. Yep, the clue is in the word, tension, part of the term hypertension. Benson's patients needed to access a state of relaxation rather than a state of tension. Benson's argument is the more someone trains themselves to arouse their rest and repair state by triggering the PNS, the more likely, they enjoy a balanced state of being, allowing tension to decrease and instead, a sense of wellbeing to actually be experienced in the body. Sensing safety and wellbeing is what the ANS needs, so that you can recalibrate and recover. You will literally benefit physically and emotionally by giving yourself time to learn to relax.

When we relax our bodies and minds after feeling agitated or anxious, we elicit what Benson termed *The Relaxation Response*. In this more laidback state, our brainwaves become longer (Alpha Waves), our heart rate slows to a healthier range, our breathing slows down, our blood pressure decreases and a greater sense of calm and wellbeing pervades. Benson studied Zen Buddhists and Yogis in deep relaxation during their meditation or lying down in Yoga relaxation and found all these physiological relaxation indicators.

The Relaxation Response is the condition which one needs to elicit for physical, emotional and mental healing to occur. The Relaxation Response is the opposite of the stress response created by the SNS. Benson and his team extrapolated from their survey of human subjects that rest and the Relaxation Response are an 'altered state' because this relaxed state is not the daily norm for most human beings. The state 'must be purposefully and consciously evoked' to arouse the good feelings associated with the PNS (Benson, 81, 1975) by following specific steps in this order: find a quiet environment to practise in, silent repetition of a mental device such as a word, sound or phrase, 'a passive attitude' and a comfortable position for the body. These steps are the blueprint from many ancient meditation practices and for evoking the state of yoga nidrā. Consciously relaxing the mind and body with practices, such as deep relaxation for yoga nidrā, awakens your PNS's power to create calm. A calm body and mind help us to recover from the physiological impact that sexual violence has had upon the ANS. We must not demonise the SNS as the bad fairy or parade the PNS as the good fairy within the ANS. Both systems contribute toward our wellbeing by letting us protect ourselves from danger, if need be, while enjoying a generally calm experience of life, if these systems are functioning in a healthy manner.

Autonomy is a core value for me and feeling that you have autonomy is crucial for your recovery process. The phrase 'passive attitude' could be interpreted as suggesting we do not have autonomy or power during relaxation exercises or yoganidrā. Rest assured, you absolutely have both autonomy and power. The term 'passive attitude' can feel more attractive when given the label 'easy going attitude' meaning that while you are resting in deep relaxation, you do not have to worry about how it is going or if you are getting it right. Instead you are taking the practice with a laidback mind-set just for the duration of the session. This non-critical, laidback attitude that you can practise during relaxation sessions is a step towards the self-compassion, which we survivors need to cultivate.

Recovery Guidance for this Week

This week's deep relaxation for welcoming Yoganidrā is intended to help you plant the seeds to anchor your recovery and to elicit your body's capacity for relaxation. I guide you through a breathing exercise and systemic relaxation technique for relaxing your body and mind.

Acknowledge your Progress:

At the end of this week, note down at least two bits of progress that are relevant to your recovery.

Five Minutes of Self-Care: Healing Herbs and Benevolent Breath

If you have a particular herb you enjoy the smell of (I like thyme), find some of your favourite herb outdoors or at a shop, snip off a few bits, rub it between your palms and slowly breathe in the scent. If you like, try this with some rose oil if you have some or pick some up inexpensively at a health shop. This is a good practice to try if you notice yourself feeling wound up or stressed. When you inhale and exhale slowly and deeply, you are sending both breath and energy over your vagus nerve and its circuit known as the ventral vagal pathway. This pathway is key to recovery and stimulating the body's Relaxation Response because it has 'an inhibitory influence' (Dr. Gail Parker, 86, 2020) that causes the heartbeat to regulate and stop it from racing.

chapter 7

WEEK TWO:

YOU DID NOT DESERVE IT AND IT WAS NOT YOUR FAULT—RECOVERING FROM NEGATIVE SELF-TALK.

> You did not deserve it and it was not Your Fault.
>
> There. I've said it. Sadly, a lot of survivors of rape think that they did deserve it and that somehow it was their fault. Many survivors attempt to normalise and minimise the fact that a person/persons had sex with them or touched them without consent. It is not normal; it is unacceptable and it is a crime. This week's words offer some relief from negative thoughts or beliefs you may be experiencing. This week's guided meditation will help you relax into compassionate self-talk.

In our day-to-day life our brains are often chock-full with thoughts. Thoughts like, '*What shall I eat today?*' Thoughts like, '*I must go for a jog one of these days.*' Thoughts like, '*If I was richer/cleverer/prettier/thinner/curvier/funnier/more organised/more confident/more go-getting, then I'd be happy.*' The brain can be a quagmire of unhelpful thoughts like this third example, and then our ego (the little voice that tells us these unhelpful thoughts and wants to keep us free from danger) berates us daily for not having gone for that jog. Before long, we believe that we are bad/lazy/unmotivated for not jogging. Beliefs are thoughts we keep on thinking. Beliefs are not the truth. So, on an average day, we believe unhelpful, unkind, untrue thoughts about ourselves. Now let's throw in the circumstance of being raped and sexually abused repeatedly and consider what kind of thoughts might be on repeat in the mind.

In the days after being attacked, I'm sure I barely had one non-negative thought. Honestly, I can barely remember doing any thinking in the hours afterwards. I felt something between numb and dry, like somebody had dried out the moisture from my brain, sucked the life from it. I know I was either staring into middle distance or asleep. Sleep is one of the ways that the brain tries to recover from and assimilate an event that triggers the body's trauma response. Events like rape can trigger feelings of numbness and physical reactions like untold tiredness. However, if you're reading this and you have not been able to sleep since being attacked, this is very usual too. Bodies process trauma in different ways.

It wasn't long before the brain's unkind thoughts started seeping in and for a while I believed these thoughts. I thought I should have seen the attack coming. I thought I should have known not to trust that man. I thought it was my fault I was raped because I'd taken drugs that night. I thought I should have run away sooner, run away faster. These thoughts were my own version of, '*I must have deserved it,*' and '*It's my fault it happened.*' Believing these thoughts was a downward spiral into believing that I didn't deserve to recover, but instead, that I deserved to feel shame and guilt for what I perceived was *my fault.* I talk more about getting free from shame in Week Six.

Perhaps, you will recognise some of the negative thoughts and beliefs, which I will list shortly; thoughts and beliefs that get triggered by rape. All these examples are different versions of *I deserved it* and *it's my fault it happened.* Before you read through the negative thoughts that sexual violence survivors may experience, this is what I want you to know: You are a good person. It was not your fault. You deserve better. You can heal from this. You are beautiful and whole. You are valuable and you matter. You are a rose. Inside you lives a very potent, ever-unfolding rose and that rose is very much alive. You made it. You are reading these words because that rose lives inside the temple of your heart and wants you to thrive. Put your hands over you heart and let these words seep in. You do not have to believe my words, but these words, my love, are the universal truths for those on the recovery path.

Here goes: *I can't believe I let this happen. Why couldn't I run away? Why couldn't I fight? I just let him or her or them do it to me. I had a gut feeling about that person or those people and I ignored it. I wish I hadn't been drunk. What should I do? What should I have done differently? I should have seen this coming. I should have known better than to walk home in the dark. I shouldn't have worn that outfit. It wasn't as bad as I remember it. It doesn't matter. I will just get on with things. I should just be able to get on with things. Why can't I get on with things? I'm fine. My life is ruined. I'm dirty now. People will know just by looking at me. I will lose my job. I will go mad if I start talking about this. I'm too angry. I can just forget about it. People have been through far worse. I won't be believed. There's no point in telling the Police. I've remembered it wrongly. He or she or they didn't mean it. He or she or they just made a mistake. He or she or they won't do it again. If he or she or they say sorry it will make it all better. God says that we need to forgive people. I should just get over it because people go through far worse. My feelings are not important. Who will take care of my children? If I start crying I know I will never stop. Crying is weak. I can never trust anyone again. The world is not safe. It is not rape because we're in a relationship. It wasn't rape because we are married. I can't leave this relationship. What will my family say? I have nobody I can talk too. I don't need to speak about it. I need to go back to work ASAP. I must keep busy. I'm weak because I couldn't fight. Why didn't I scream? I will never be able to have sex again. I can't tell my partner. What if I get blamed? What's wrong with me? I'm a bad person. I hate myself. I hate my body. I'm not going to be able to cope. I must stay strong. How come I didn't die? Will I end up taking anti-depressants or anti-anxiety drugs?*

Before we move on, let me say again: You are a good person. It was not your fault. You deserve better. You can heal from this. You are beautiful and whole. You are valuable and you matter. You are a rose. Inside you lives a very potent, ever-unfolding rose and that rose is very much alive. You made it. You are reading these words because that rose lives inside the temple of your heart and wants you to thrive.

'The Only Way Out is Through'
– Alanis Morissette, Singer-Songwriter

I promise you that you do not need to be afraid of negative thoughts. Just because your brain is having them, it does not mean that these thoughts are true or that you must act on them. Unhelpful thoughts, which tell us we are stupid or dirty or useless or damaged or somehow the world would be better if we were not in it at all, come from a place that some people call 'the Shadow.' Some people say the Shadow is destructive. I disagree. I say that the Shadow not recognised as a Shadow looms large because the ego (the voice in our head that questions and judges EVERYTHING) hooks into it to confirm that we are in danger. Listening to our ego can spiral us into despair and depression because the ego searches for evidence to fuel its lust for fear. If left unnoticed, the ego will continue to drag one into a life filled with fear. Fear is the opposite of thriving. If we fail to intervene in the ego's spiral of fear-driven thinking, that is when things tend to become 'destructive' and people can end up doing self-harm behaviours like getting wrecked on alcohol, drugs or cutting (I know all three very well) in an attempt to ease or distract from the pain of such thinking. Even now, I see these destructive acts as coping mechanisms, which helped me with the struggle, as I used to see it, of being alive. If you have been cutting or getting wrecked, I get it; it can help let the pain out, but there are safer ways of coping, if you want to try some. A therapist can really be supportive to you in finding new ways to cope and work through the hurt that we feel we have had to live with. When I was breaking the habit of cutting, I would try to remember to hold an ice cube, rather than pick up a sharp object, to release the rage pent up inside that I felt unable to face safely.

The Shadow part of ourselves is not an aspect that we need to shun or hide from. Instead, we can make an ally of our Shadow and let it show us the pain we need to feel and move through. If we can allow ourselves to feel safe and at ease by trying some kind of meditation practice or by chatting with a kind friend, we can voice our Shadow and let it speak with us. As a woman, it is very much in our collective conditioning that we be nice, whereas voicing the words of our Shadow wouldn't make us sound very nice. Proclaiming that we are angry as hell and feel like getting blind drunk, and not under the façade of fun, but to forget our problems, that it seems like a good idea to burn down Parliament and that we feel like seeing the person/persons who attacked us rot in jail all come from the Shadow. Now, the Shadow is your friend. The Shadow wants our rage, outrage and howling to be heard, to be seen and known. The Shadow wants us to scream, for all around to hear, "Why the fuck did this happen to me?!" The Shadow is the untamed version of you that life has tried to tame. From my perspective as a survivor, our Shadow can be our greatest ally for recovery. Our Shadow lets us witness and feel our authentic pain without being destroyed by it. Your Shadow wants you to recover and live your life. My Shadow is helping me write this book.

You are not bad or wrong or silly or melodramatic for having any of these thoughts like, *'I'm stupid'* or *'I hate everyone/myself.'* The brain makes up thoughts on its own because it is the brain's job to overthink. Same as it is our heart's job to circulate blood, the brain's job is to circulate thoughts. The more unhelpful thinking that happens, the more of these thoughts that go around and around and around. Believing the brain's thoughts is an unkind thing to do to yourself when you have experienced a trauma. You deserve maximum kindness right now (and all the time) so we must begin by doing what we can do to show compassion to ourselves. Would you say any of the above things to a person who told you they had been raped? I thought not. You definitely do not have to believe your own brain's bad press or berate yourself for something that you did not deserve and that was not your fault.

It is also very possible that you have not had any thoughts about it being your fault or deserving it; and if you have, you haven't necessarily believed these thoughts. If this is you, I am so glad. You might have realised that these thoughts belong with nasty lies and myths that some Stone Age people say about survivors of rape. Sometimes, lies like these can end up as collective beliefs held by groups or whole societies and somehow end up infiltrating our own psyches. You do not need to buy these lies about being shamed or blamed as a rape survivor. You made it through. You did what you did to survive. You get to take care of yourself, you get to recover, you get to heal and you get to celebrate yourself again sooner or later: Your recovery, your pace.

So how can we help ourselves to notice what kind of thinking the brain is doing? Is it compassionate thinking or unhelpful thinking?

Meditation can help us to feel safe and not totally overwhelmed by unhelpful thoughts. I have been meditating regularly for about 10 years, and so I already had a steady practice and was able to call on this blessing of a recovery tool in the weeks after the attack. Meditation has a few different forms, but it was mindfulness meditation that was most helpful in letting me observe my brain's thoughts circling around and around. Many people think that meditation is about stopping thoughts from happening, as if we must sit there in silence and empty our mind and focus on not thinking. Not true. Meditation helps us be with or 'witness' the thoughts that we are having, without getting sucked into the whirlpool of unhelpful thinking, which takes us towards false beliefs about ourselves, beliefs about being stupid or guilty and thoughts like, '*I should have known better.*' We are enabled to have these unhelpful thoughts without being blindsided by them, to be with the thoughts happening and come through them. Alanis Morissette sings in her song, '*The Only Way Out Is Through*,' 'My urgency to dream of softer places feels understandable, but the only way out is through.' I invite you to try some meditation. Many people report that regular meditation helps them foster feelings of self-compassion. If you think meditation is not for you, that's cool, but you have nothing to lose by giving it a quick go.

Recovery Ritual: Mindfulness Meditation

This is a very gentle path into meditation. Over time, meditation shows us that we are not our thoughts and beliefs.

Sit comfortably or lie down in a place where you won't be disturbed. Set a timer for five minutes.

Close your eyes, or if this feels disconcerting, focus your gaze downwards. Sit in silence for 10 seconds, staying in your comfortable position.

After 10 seconds, notice your breath entering your nostrils and leaving your nostrils. Softly, guide your attention on to your breath. Count one on the inhale, two on the exhale, three on the next inhale and so on until you reach 10. When your mind gets distracted and you realise you're having thoughts, gently guide your attention back to your breath and start again, counting from one. Continue until the timer sounds.

When the timer sounds, let go of your effort, give up trying to follow the breath or noticing being distracted. Instead, just let the mind be free for a few seconds. You can also find this meditation recorded for you in the *Shadow and Rose* area on my website (www.youreenoughyoga.com).

What you say about yourself matters because your words reinforce what you believe about yourself. There is a neuroscientific theory summarised as, 'Neurons that fire together, wire together.' So the more you repeat a neural circuit, such as the circuit of negative self-talk, the stronger that circuit becomes. The more we repeat a behaviour pattern, the more neural connections our brains literally create that are more solid, reinforcing this trait or habit. These ingrained neural circuits mean these ingrained unhelpful patterns happen automatically and are often harder to break. This is true for the human go-to pattern of talking about ourselves harshly or judgementally. Talking about ourselves without the harsh edge takes practice but is absolutely possible. Be patient with your brain as it starts to shift its wiring and as it creates new wiring for kinder self-talk.

We cast spells with our words because words have the energy of intention behind them. For example, if I am feeling bad about myself for some reason, it is unhelpful for me to say to myself or anyone else, something like, *'I'm such a loser. I shouldn't feel sad like this. I'm supposed to know better.'* Firstly, this is an untrue statement because nobody told me I should know better; only the voice of my inner critic, whom I like to call *Shirty Shirley*. Secondly, I only reinforce my low mood by saying a statement of judgement about myself like this one. Statements like these are spells, which we inadvertently cast upon ourselves, that spiral us deeper into feelings of unworthiness and upset. This being said, it is very important that you do not deny your feelings, suppress them nor try to make them more palatable for people to hear, by being positive. Positivity is powerful and has its place, but not when it is a cover-up for you expressing what is really going on for you emotionally. With self-compassion and lots of practising talking about myself more kindly, my above statement might go like this, "I am feeling sad and I am judging myself harshly for feeling like this." Can you hear that this version is kinder and less attacking toward my already upset self? The self, who is the younger smaller version of me, is having a hard time.

What about the stuff you are saying to yourself? Let a pen write it out through you, talk it out of you with a therapist, let your tears cry it out of you, stamp it into the ground with your feet. If you walk, run, dance or hike, let it seep out of you into the earth as you unlearn the frenzied mental activity and learn to treat yourself well. Let it teach you that you deserve better from yourself.

Recovery Ritual: Burn it up

Set a timer for between five and 10 minutes and simply write out, without a care in the world as to whether it makes sense, the unkind things you say to yourself as a result of sexual violence you experienced or any other generally unkind self-talk you say to yourself. In a safe place, for example, over your sink or somewhere with water nearby, light a match and set fire to the paper with the harmful words you have written down. Watch the paper turn into ash and the energy of your words burn up into the ether for release. Put the burning paper under the tap or in water when you feel ready (and before it gets too risky for the environment you are in!) Place your hands on your heart and mentally say any words of comfort to yourself, such as, "It was not my fault and I deserve so much better."

SHADOW AND ROSE

'A great deal depends upon the thought patterns we choose and the persistence with which we affirm them.'
— **Piero Ferrucci, Psychotherapist**

Recovery Guidance for this Week

This week's yoga nidrā is intended to help you cultivate feelings of self-compassion.

Acknowledge your Progress:

At the end of this week, note down at least two bits of progress that are relevant to your recovery.

Five Minutes of Self-Care:

Sit quietly. Breathe in slowly through your nose. Breathe out very slowly through your nose. Enjoy the quiet. Place your non-dominant hand on your heart while you write down five things you appreciate about yourself. Stick this list up on your mirror or keep it in your purse.

chapter 8

WEEK THREE:

MORE THAN JUST A SPA DAY— RECOVERING YOUR RIGHT TO SELF-CARE

> **Make Your Own Recovery Your Only Priority in Life**
>
> How do you feel when you read that statement? Take five to 10 minutes to sit quietly and journal your response.

In the first weeks after being raped, I really did not like myself very much. Taking care of myself was lower than low on my priority list. I thought that I didn't deserve to care for myself, that if I ever felt compassion and care again, it would have to come from somebody else, rather than directed from me to me. Most of my life, I had been relying on other people to love and care for me, and since I had been sexually violated, I believed my unkind thought that nobody would ever love me again. Once again, thanks to therapy, not only did I begin to unpick this strongly held false belief, I also connected with the crucial practice of self-care for the very first time.

Growing up, I had always had an uneasy relationship with myself and often felt I wasn't good enough. I know from sharing and chatting with friends and other survivors, I am not alone in this experience. We have been miseducated and conditioned by unhealthy messages, which never highlight our right to nurture and love ourselves. These messages are often fed into us through parenting and miseducation. Usually parents do mean well, yet through their own unconsciousness and conditioning from their parents, they end up feeding us with some giant, red flag false beliefs, stemming from their own skewed relationship to self-care.

Going through school, we get drilled on how to do quadratic equations and how to organise a fluent essay, but where were the lessons about how to nourish and care for ourselves? Lessons based in assessing our own needs were non-existent. The vibe from teachers in my own secondary school was that you could always improve. No grade was ever good enough and the closest we came to being taught how to care for ourselves were a few clumsy lessons from flustered teachers on personal hygiene and puberty, which boiled down to advice to wear a deodorant so as not to smell or offend people with the body's natural smell (yep, body shaming starts young). Rewind to a few years earlier and children, who went to Brownies, like I did, were taught to promise to '*Always put others before myself.*' Reciting this promise was part of the swearing in ceremony to become a Brownie. At the age of seven, witnessed by other little girls and grown-ups, I unwittingly made a verbal contract to put other people's needs before my own. This was how I lived my life, pouring from an exhausted, empty vessel.

I never took time to take real care of myself. I don't mean the self-care like going to the hairdresser every couple of months, or for a spa day – which are all good, by the way – but the self-care that sees one be still, rest and listen to one's own guidance about our wants and needs, saying "No" to invitations and "No" to that friend, who is always needing our attention when we need rest the most.

When was the last time you said "No" to an invite or to helping somebody out AND did not feel the need to justify your No with a convincing reason? Saying "No" is a form of self-care.

I never stopped to consider that the work I did, the favours I offered, the extra mile I went in friendships nourished everybody but me. I was sure that one day my friends would realise that I wasn't worth being around and would soon abandon me and I was convinced any opportunities which came my way would be pulled out from under my feet. So, to stay ahead and appear to be a good woman I did what seven-year-old Sarah had promised and I continued to, 'Always put other people before myself.' My guard was always up, and it was exhausting. After I was raped, the volume dial of this lifelong exhaustion and Imposter Syndrome amplified. There was something else creeping in this time, alongside the anxiety. I felt scorn toward myself for failing, as I perceived it, to protect myself from the attack, scorn toward the rapist and scorn that I now had something else epic to recover from in addition to PTSD, which my therapist had diagnosed the previous year.

I felt that something vital had been stolen from me when my body was violated. I didn't know what it was but I knew something was missing. I never precisely articulated what it was, but when my therapist chimed in that nobody deserves to have their enjoyment of life stolen by a rapist, this deeply resonated for me. I was shutting myself down from life, letting myself go numb, in fear of having to feel anything like the pain of what I went through that night, which had become enmeshed with the shame I felt at already having experienced sexual violence. I oscillated between numbness, shame, bitterness, hopelessness and rage. Sometimes these feelings were aimed at the world, but usually it was me these emotions were aimed at. I was starting to believe that I did not deserve to recover. However, with ongoing clinical support and therapy, meditation and the self-care practices listed in this book, I uncovered the truth; I am worth the time needed to recover and I deserve a good life. So do you.

Recovery Ritual: Spotting Self-Care Gremlins

Sit quietly in a space where you feel safe and will not be disturbed. If you choose to do this at home, perhaps light a candle to mark this moment.

Set a timer for five minutes and write out the things that stop you from really caring for yourself. These may be false beliefs, words from other people, your hectic schedule, your family, feelings of shame and things connected with your experience of sexual violence. These are your gremlins or blocks to your self-care.

Naming what stops our self-care helps us make conscious choices about how we wish to nurture ourselves from now on.

Here is a list with some ideas of how you can care for yourself as you recover:

- **Ask for help from professionals** who are trained to support survivors of sexual violence (see the contacts list at the back of the book).

- **Consider seeing your GP if you feel your mental health is suffering.** They may ask if you want to be prescribed medication to help ease you through anxiety or looming depression. Taking medications for mental health is a totally personal choice and I chose to do so. I took a very low dose of an anti-anxiety drug for about three months, which helped me feel like I could face the impact of being raped and its effect on my mind, body and spirit. Again, it's your recovery process and your choice about how you choose to recover and nurture your mental health. I looked at taking medications as an extra helping hand or buffer towards recovering my bearings in life. As survivors, we deserve all the help we can get and medication is one source of help for you if you choose it. There are of course herbal alternatives to doctor prescribed anti anxiety drugs and antidepressants. Some commonly used herbals to calm the mood are Ashwagandha, St John's Wort and a host of other natural remedies that can be recommended by a qualified herbalist or homeopath. Always check whether herbal alternatives could negatively affect any prescribed medication you are already taking.

- **Move your body with nourishing exercise.** What exercise you consider nourishing for you may be different from another survivor's nourishing exercise. It's very subjective. I am saying this because you don't need to feel like you should go jogging, if you hate jogging. If you feel more depleted than nourished after circuit training, then perhaps leave that out for a while. I spent days in bed after I was attacked and this is very normal. Eventually, my body wanted to move but it simply did not want to go running which had previously been my go-to exercise alongside yoga. It wanted something gentler so I upped my yoga practice and took myself out for a walk when I felt like it. If you are craving a good run though, go for it! Just be mindful that in early recovery, you may need to nourish yourself more than exhaust yourself. Your body is relying on you to treat it kindly so you can heal. Too much vigorous exercise too often can push the SNS into a heightened state, making it much trickier for your PNS to do its calming work.

- **Drop some essential oils into a warm bath.** I like to use one drop of rose oil or one drop of lavender, mixed with a carrier oil, like coconut oil because it is neutral. Always use a carrier oil if, like me, you have sensitive skin. Be sparing with essential oils, they are rather a trend but over use can be harmful.

- **Meditation** - again, sorry to any of you, who are convinced that meditation will not work for you. I am not suggesting that you start off with 20 minutes sitting bolt upright on a pillow trying to clear your mind every day. Starting with one minute is enough. As I have mentioned, meditation is not about clearing or emptying the mind, although this is a common misconception. Meditation is about giving us room to be with what is happening instead of trying to change what is happening. For example, accepting that you feel agitated, while sitting quietly for one or two minutes, is kinder than trying to force yourself to stop feeling agitated by doing a long meditation and feeling it's not working because you are agitated; and getting increasingly agitated because you perceive it is not working! When we give ourselves a little time and space to acknowledge our mental state, these less pleasant states often fade into the background, allowing us to go about our day feeling less uptight. Those of us who have trauma may find it harder to sit and meditate than people who do not have trauma, so be sweet to yourself about this. Remember that mindful movement such as mindful yoga and somatic movement practices also count as meditation.

- **Buy yourself some roses or flowers of your choice.** The energy of flowers and plants is so healing; even just glancing at a vase of roses for a moment can awaken joy. You deserve all the joy and beauty.

- **Consider drinking less booze.** Alcohol is a complex topic. If you feel you may be drinking too much, you may like to approach a support group like Alcoholics Anonymous. Alcohol is both depressant and suppressant so it has a nasty habit of making us feel worse when we were not feeling good to begin with; a bit like a toxic friend, who somehow makes us feel even more down after chatting with them. Only you can know if your relationship with alcohol is problematic or if you are using it as too much of a crutch to handle the complex and sometimes frightening emotions, which may get stirred up by our recovery from a trauma like sexual violence. It is fully understandable that you may want to drink more than usual when you are recovering. It does not mean you are doing something bad or weak, but where possible, notice if drinking makes you feel better or worse in the bigger picture; and not just while you are drinking. Trust me, I wanted to reach for the vodka and diet coke daily and sometimes, I did, but over time, drinking a bit less actually helped me to feel more stable.

- **Try a Reiki Session.** Yes, I am biased because I am a Reiki Practitioner and Master/ Teacher! Please indulge me on this one. Like yoga, Reiki is a spiritual system of its own and is intended to allow people to reconnect with their true selves, melting away the layers of crummy beliefs and self-doubt that can leave people feeling depressed and their body suffering. Similar to the eight-limbed yoga path, Reiki has five branches or limbs, but Reiki is most widely known for the branch we call healing. This aspect of Reiki enables me as the practitioner to share the energy of Reiki to myself for self-healing (which is how I start most of my days with a little self-healing Reiki session) and to other people should they consent to receiving Reiki for their own healing. People turn to Reiki to help them recover and manage pain from physical injuries, unexplained body pains and chronic conditions like ME (Myalgic Encephalomyelitis), to convalesce following operations and also to support them with mental health issues, recovery from trauma or deepening their spiritual connection with whatever the higher power they believe in. A higher power doesn't necessarily refer to God or some other deity, but can be the connection to your own highest/truest self. Some people might call this the soul. I first encountered Reiki, which roughly translates as universal life force energy, when I was piecing my health and emotions back together while in my early days of anorexia recovery after exiting a domestic abuse relationship. A friend of mine, who I am eternally grateful for, mentioned to me that she got attuned to Reiki while growing up in Hong Kong and offered me a short session on a day when my anxiety was running me ragged. I had no clue what attuned meant or what Reiki actually referred to, but I trusted her after years of friendship, so I agreed. She placed one hand very lightly on my forehead and the other on the crown of my head. Instantly, I felt calm. After a few minutes she placed her hands on my shoulders. The best way I can describe the sensation was like a warm wave of peace passing over and through my body.

The sense of safety and calm I felt from the Reiki energy and the care of my friend, who was a closet Reiki Practitioner, left me feeling like the experience had ignited a part of myself that I had not felt before. This was my body's healing mechanism being coaxed awake by the benevolent energy of Reiki. You do not have to be touched to receive Reiki, you can have a hands-off session where the practitioner works around your aura (the space which hovers above the physical body) or you can have a remote session where you are not even in the same building as the Reiki practitioner. Some of my clients say they find these remote sessions the most powerful and calming. Everyone is different though so, in your own time, if you want to try Reiki, choose the kind of session that feels right for you.

- **Eat Yourself Toward Recovery.** I did not want to eat in the early days after I was raped. My nervous system was all over the place and so, my appetite was suppressed by the SNS's high alert state and my body struggled to digest anything I did eat. In addition to these usual responses of the SNS, I had a relapse of the insidious, unkind thoughts towards myself that were edging me once again in the direction of Anorexia-Town, toward starvation and food restriction.

Illnesses like eating disorders (anorexia, bulimia, eating disorder not otherwise specified or overeating) sometimes get triggered into existence or relapse due to acts of sexual violence. If you think this could be happening to you, check out the resource page at the back of this book.

Disclaimer! I am not a dietician but these food options continue to support my own recovery. If you are feeling stressed, you might like to eat food that is cooling for the body such as avocados, berries, asparagus in cold dishes, like salads or smoothies, and add in a type of carbohydrate that your body will tolerate. Consider avoiding white carbs because these are so hard for the body to digest and often leave women feeling really sluggish. Be sure to switch the cooling food for warm dishes too, like simple soups or stews. Honouring your recovery by giving yourself good whole food makes for a good self-care habit. The types of food, which a female body really needs, varies from woman to woman and from week to week due to our nature as cyclical beings, as we are much less likely to feel the same from day-to-day. Women have a body rhythm called the infradian rhythm, which lasts a 28-day cycle and is felt most strongly by women, who have not yet begun menopause. Honouring the infradian rhythm is also important for women who are in menopause. It is very helpful for female health if you connect consciously with the infradian rhythm rather than the 24-hour cycle of the circadian rhythm (the one in which you operate on a 24-hour cycle of the same activities every day. This is the cycle that male wellness is connected to and it works well for men. It's like a rinse and repeat cycle). Women are not rinse and repeat creatures and our emotions, moods, dietary needs, energy levels and hormones are designed to vary from week to week. For a game-changing insight and coaching on living in harmony with the infradian rhythm, check out Alissa Vitti's website, (www.flowliving.com) or get hold of a copy of her seminal, scientifically informed book, *In the Flo*.

- **Try Some Yoga.** YYoga helps the mind and body to feel more spacious, while also letting people drop out of their habitual thought patterns into a calmer state. If Yoga is not your thing, perhaps try Qi Gong, or martial arts or dance as a type of nourishing, mindful bodywork.

- **Walk Outdoors In Nature.** Whenever you feel ready to go for a wander, I cannot emphasise enough the healing potential of being outside connecting with nature. Nature is accessible everywhere, whether you notice the greenery on our streets, hear a bird singing in the morning, tend to a house plant, or even go for a walk along the seafront on a blustery day. Soil contains nutrients and aromas that when smelled, promote the production of dopamine to encourage feelings of relaxation.

Recovery Guidance for this Week

This week's guided relaxation is intended to help you cultivate a self-care practice by choosing a 'Sankalpa', which is a committed, heart-based resolve to underpin your recovery.

Acknowledge your Progress:

At the end of this week, note down at least two bits of progress that are relevant to your recovery.

Five Minutes of Self-Care:

Write out your Recovery Sankalpa, decorate this paper with doodles or drawings, anything to make it pretty. Keep it in your purse.

chapter 9

WEEK FOUR:

SAYING YES TO YOURSELF—RECOVERING YOUR BOUNDARIES AND VOICE

Boundaries and Self-Care are best friends, they go hand-in-hand and help us to reclaim a sense of both stability and personal power in the aftermath of being sexually attacked. This week's words and guided relaxation will help you to connect more deeply to your sense of self, your right to discern what kind of behaviour you allow in your life, while keeping your needs at the forefront of your recovery. When we implement boundaries as an act of self-care, we protect our energy and peace of mind from being drained by the words and actions of other people. Setting and voicing boundaries can feel

> daunting at first and require you to behave in a way that you are not used to, so that you can put your own needs and recovery before the needs of other people. Healthy boundaries transform our lives and shift us from victim mode into a Fiercely Loving Autonomous Bad Ass. Yep, that description belongs on a T-shirt!

I grew up as an only child and so I had no siblings to practise boundary setting with when I was young. I don't really mind because I liked being an only child, but I think I missed out somewhat on knowing how to say "yes" and "no" in response to people about what behaviour I was OK with from them and what presented a no-go. I would go over to my friends' houses and see them fighting with their siblings when a brother or sister ate the last of their Maltesers or sat on their bit of the sofa watching *Neighbours*. I was quite a timid child and all this shouting and pushing around that I saw seemed a bit intense for me, but what was happening was that my friends were exercising their right to their personal boundaries and effectively communicating yes or no to what they liked or didn't like; albeit it in an appropriately chaotic and literally childlike fashion. I remember being in junior school and a 'friend' was horrible to me and stole my necklace. I was clueless about what to do or how to say and show that ignoring me for a few days and then stealing from me was really out of order. I hadn't been able to rehearse these boundary conflict situations with siblings and so I kept silent and felt embarrassed. I felt queasy that somebody I knew had taken what was mine and that I couldn't do anything about it. This is one of my earliest experiences of a personal boundary violation. My childhood friend had no right to invade, no responsibility for, nor ownership of my personal space and necklace, and yet invaded my space and took what belonged to me. Tangible or physical boundaries are all around us. We see fences, gates, doors, the central reservation on the motorway; these all show us where one thing ends and another begins. The gate on a driveway shows that whatever is inside that gate belongs to a person and that that person is responsible for and owns that property. Nobody else has a right to, responsibility for, nor ownership of that property. The other side of the gate marks where the pavement is; the homeowner is not responsible for and does not own that section of pavement. Our skin is like a gate, keeping the boundary of our physical bodies. We are responsible for ourselves and have ownership over our bodies. Nobody else has a right to your body, nobody else is responsible for your body and certainly nobody else owns your body. You are a Sovereign woman who has a right to boundaries, a responsibility for your boundaries and ownership of your Self. Our skin is a tangible boundary marker, like a gate, that shows the outer edge or boundary of the physical body. But it is also possible to experience a boundary having been overstepped when somebody comes too close to our personal space, without being touched physically. When I was training in Reiki I learned a lot about the energy field that surrounds a person's physical body. There are many layers to this energy field. On the outside of the physical body we have tiers of energy that still belong to us; one of these layers is called the aura. Whether you believe in these invisible energy fields or not, they do exist, and we can feel ours when somebody stands that little bit too close to us. Our energy field detects the sensation of another physical body being close to ours, and then the brain sorts through information in lightening quick speed to assess whether we are in danger or not. In the immediate days after being sexually assaulted I struggled to have any person near me, as not only my body but also my energy field had been invaded and disrupted by the attack. I would start to sweat walking along a pavement if a man even looked in my direction, let alone walked near me on the same side of the street. I was not into hugs from anyone for a while either because this felt too close to my physical boundary, which had been so massively disrespected.

My mind and body reacted this way due to the physiological symptoms of trauma. Trauma can be deactivated when it is addressed by professional therapists who know how to help the survivor down-regulate their nervous system. This can be a slow process, but this is OK, because you are at the heart of your healing and when you move at your own pace in the recovery process, this is you taking ownership of your recovery, setting boundaries and being autonomous.

You have the right to voice what physical behaviour is acceptable or unacceptable. You have the right to voice a hard, absolute "Fuck Off, No!" However, our right to, responsibility for and ownership of our boundaries may feel utterly wrecked after suffering any kind of abuse or sexual violence.

Re-establishing and setting boundaries has been an integral part of my recovery by allowing me to recover my autonomy. I felt I had no autonomy and no voice to speak out with after I was raped. I had said "No" to somebody having sex with me, I had tried to fight him off, and still it happened. I was frightened that anything else I would ever say "No" to would be ignored leaving me with no say, no voice. I felt that my voice had been stolen along with my right to say "yes" or "no," and in these early stages of recovery I felt helpless, hopeless and powerless. The more I came to understand, believe and know that none of it was my fault, the safer I felt in the validity of my boundaries and with the voice to speak up for myself. My boundaries and voice were always completely valid and powerful, but the mind trick of sex crimes is the survivor being made to feel like they have no power, no strength to heal their life. Sex crimes are the ultimate case in point of breaking another person's boundaries. Sexual violence is a perfect storm, which violates our physical, emotional and mental boundaries. Remember how I laid it out for you earlier and said that, "**You did not deserve it and it was not your fault?**" That was me reminding you that being sexually abused, assaulted and/or raped is indefensible behaviour and nobody should be expected to tolerate this behaviour. The very nature of being sexually attacked is that we did not want it to happen and so this attack is an absolute boundary violation. Whether you were able to scream out, "No" or "Stop" or "Fuck Off," or whether you were stunned into frozen silence when you were attacked is irrelevant, your body, mind and heart did not want to be sexually interfered with. Survivors of sexual violence often feel completely boundary-less and powerless in the aftermath.

I wanted to shut myself away from people after I was raped. I literally packed some stuff, left London, which had been my home for 10 years and went to stay with my parents. I knew it wouldn't be forever because I loved London, but I honestly could not fathom being in the same city as the man who raped me. I was frightened he would find me somehow, and even though I had reported the crime to the Police, any sense of feeling safe had been dragged unceremoniously and suddenly from under my feet. This gnawing sense of fear and lack of security is usual for survivors; some of the women I met in group therapy felt like this too. I had not been able to protect myself when I was attacked and so, I was adamant that I would do anything I could to protect myself from being harmed ever again. Going out on my own? No thanks. Drinking with friends in pubs? Forget it. Letting a man anywhere near me ever again? Absolutely not. I was putting up barriers around me.

Barriers and boundaries are not the same things. Barriers are driven by fear, isolation and turning away from life. Boundaries are fuelled by self-care, they are flexible if we want them to be and they help us grow and heal so that life can be enjoyable again. Over time, I started to realise that I did not want to shut down or be hidden in the shadows of life, succumbing to the heartbreak. I had survived and so I still had a life; a life, which was mine to enjoy. Bit by bit, I put myself at the centre of my life because recovering was all that mattered. As part of my recovery plan from my therapist, I meditated more often, which actually only meant two 10-minute sessions each day. This might not sound very much but my nervous system was too jumpy to be able to even sit still in silence for two minutes at a time in the early days of recovery. The more often I let myself sit in silence in these prescribed meditation sessions, just being quiet with myself, the more I connected with an inner sense of safety. Meditation was helping me to trust life and to trust that I was safe. The scary stories that my brain would run on repeat about being unwanted, helpless, hopeless and powerless were still there in the background but they got quieter and some days, they would fade into the recesses completely. I knew I was recovering because I was spending less time feeling scared and more time considering new ways to heal, possibilities for my return to London, for seeing friends and having the confidence to socialise once again because there was no tattoo of the word 'victim' on my forehead for all to see. I trusted that I was capable of surviving without having to put up barriers to ensure my safety, and that I would use my blossoming sense of autonomy and trust to facilitate my participation in life.

Here are some of my examples of boundary setting, which I hope will inspire your own sense of power to bloom:

- **Taking time away from my job so that I could fully be with my emotions.** In 2017, I worked at a school on a self-employed contract, so I appreciate it may have been easier for me to take time off work than it may be for other people with less job flexibility. However, if you want to set a boundary to ring-fence time for the early stages of your recovery (and I truly encourage you to take as long as you can away from work, particularly if you work in a highly pressured environment), then you can be signed off work by your GP for mental health reasons. In the UK you will be entitled to statutory sick pay.

- **I stopped watching so much TV.** Is this boundary setting? Yep. There is an insane amount of dramatised sexual violence on TV and I just did not want to be exposed to it early on in my recovery. I did not want those images entering my psyche as a reminder of what had happened. Truthfully, a few years on, I still don't want to watch it on TV shows.

- **I negotiated with my supervisor to reduce my teaching hours** for a while, once I felt ready to return to work. I was unwilling to work a full week until the anxiety I was suffering stopped bubbling up so often. You are entitled to request a staggered return to work or reduced hours if you feel this will benefit your recovery. Eventually, it may feel like returning to work on your own terms provides you with a daily routine, reminding you of your highly capable nature and talent in whatever field you work in.

- **I didn't do anything I didn't want to do or go anywhere I didn't want to go.** . If friends invited me to go for a night out in the part of town where I was attacked (which annoyingly was the locality where our usual nights out took place), I would decline the offer. If you want to stay home where you may have been up for partying before, or don't want to go out at night with friends, just say, "No thanks." There is no need to justify or explain your choice. In time, you may want to go out on the town again. I certainly felt good about doing that when I felt ready. But until you feel ready, set your boundary and just 'do you.'

Notice that all these boundaries are flexible because I could renegotiate with myself at any time. My choices were not barriers because they all gave me room for manoeuvre while caring for myself by defining the direction and pace of my recovery. Setting your boundaries will put you in the driving seat of your recovery. You are the only one who gets to have dominion over your life. Maintaining your sovereignty is key to your healing. While you are practising the crucial art of setting boundaries, be alert to any suggestions from people that you have become selfish, boring, self-centred. Let any comments like these, subtle as they may be, function as red flag signals that you are absolutely right to set that boundary with that person. Ruffling peoples' feathers, especially on those who may have you down as the easy-going, eager to please, always available friend, is a sure sign that you are doing well at setting boundaries.

There was a time when learning about boundaries as part of self-care felt like a foreign land to me. I am eternally grateful for my therapist, who helped me to understand the importance of boundaries and gain the confidence to practise setting them. This absolutely incredible human being is Debra Kilby. Debra is an intuitive energy reader and healer, spirit baby medium and channel for the spirit. Debra has been practising energy healing since 2010. Debra is a qualified Spiritual Counsellor, Advanced Theta Healer and Advanced Soul Plan Reader. She is a member of the Holistic Healing College (HHC) and Theta Healing Institute of Knowledge. She is an expert in EFT (tapping), Matrix and Birth Matrix Reimprinting and an EFTMRA member.

Debra creates a loving and safe space for women to heal and find a deeper understanding of their life experiences, to feel confident, courageous and wholly them. Debra's website is listed in the resources section of this book.

This is what she has to say about boundaries :

"Creating boundaries is one of the greatest gifts that you can give to yourself. The sense of this is me, my body, my feelings and my choices. Feeling comfortable saying "yes" to yourself and "no" to others, whose demands, requests or energy does not fit with your own.

I see boundaries not as a form of protection, which can feel contracting and coming from fear, but as a form of permission.

Giving yourself permission to be, do and feel whatever it is you choose in every moment within your divine bubble of space. Everyone else has the exact same permission – only in their space and not yours – unless you give them permission to do so.

There are so many life experiences, going right back to your time in the womb that can influence how easy or difficult it is to create boundaries for yourself. Where you are with your boundaries can be a measure of your sense of self-worth and of how much you value yourself.

Loving yourself (and feeling worthy to do so) is one of the greatest challenges. It is also a journey to the greatest feelings of joy and freedom. You hold within, no matter how deeply buried, the courage to begin healing those moments which led you to believe that you are not worthy. As you do so, you begin to recognise you are indeed worthy of love, kindness, respect and living your heart's desires.

To know and to feel yourself move from a place of feeling disempowered into a space of self-love and self-belief. To create yourself, to respect yourself and to establish your boundaries is you rising into the beauty, love and magnificence that you are – the Truth of who you are beneath the hurt.

Just as you have a physical shower every day, it's important to wash away the energetic grime – our own and that from others. To take responsibility for what we're feeling and what we want to feel and do – our boundaries.

Say "yes" to receiving the blessing of sensitivity and the energy of the following beliefs to help you to feel more in tune with the subtle energies of the world, without your own energy being affected. Create your own boundaries.

- I have the highest truth and understanding of energy
- I know what it feels like when I am standing solely in my own energy and power
- I know what it feels like to have boundaries and to put them into place
- I know what it feels like to be safe creating my own boundaries
- I am safe
- I know what it feels like to give myself permission to be sensitive to the world of energy, without being affected by it
- I know what it feels like to respond with compassion and yet also to respond with firm boundaries
- I understand that although I may perceive all, I have the power to choose what I allow to enter my field of energy

- I know how to release energy that is not mine, to cut cords and ties that drain my own energy

- I know what it feels like to live without feeling responsible for anyone other than myself

- I know how it feels to give myself permission to release any fear, judgement or shame around any experiences of disempowerment

- I know what it feels like to trust my perception and intuition

- I know how to and I choose to live my daily life with this grace and ease now. I deserve to and I am safe in doing so.

And so it is."

Reading Debra's words reminds me of our fundamental right to boundaries. The cords she refers to above are energy cords that can have use feeling tied to traumatic experiences. You can find out more about this kind of energy healing work on Debra's website which is in the resources section at the back of this book. If you do not feel confident with boundary setting quite yet, just let yourself ponder this chapter and feel into Debra's wisdom. Try it on, see what fits and leave the rest. That process itself is discernment which is also boundary setting!

Nature has so much to teach us about keeping boundaries in place for as long as we need. Take the example of a caterpillar creating the chrysalis as its boundary, keeping itself cocooned away from the outer world, while it moves through its morphing process into a butterfly. The caterpillar is self-governing as to when it will be ready to interact with the outside world in a new form, appearing from within its chrysalis boundary. Trust your own choices about boundaries because cocooning for safety for a period of time is essential while you recover. Notice if you are being tempted to relinquish a boundary too soon because somebody else thinks you should. You are in charge of this process and when you are ready you will step out anew.

> *'Creating Boundaries Is One Of The Greatest Gifts You Can Give To Yourself'*
> **– Debra Kilby, Therapist**

Recovery Guidance for this Week

This week's guided relaxation is intended to help you connect to the physical boundary of your body and to soothe the throat, home of your sacred voice.

Acknowledge Your Progress:

At the end of this week, note down at least two bits of progress that are relevant to your recovery.

Five Minutes of Self-Care:

Write out the mantra: "Treating myself as a precious rose will make me strong." Now list five things/actions that will help you govern your boundaries.

chapter 10

 ———————————————

WEEK FIVE:

LETTING OUT STEAM— RECOVERING FROM POST-TRAUMATIC STRESS DISORDER

> In the aftermath of sexual violence it is very usual for the survivor to experience trauma. In this week's chapter, you will read about the symptoms of trauma, along with the prolonged symptoms of a mental health condition called PTSD. I also tell you about a lesser-known phenomenon called Post-Traumatic Growth (PTG). This week's yoga nidrā will support you in sowing the seeds for trauma recovery. I am not a Traumatologist or Mental Health Physician, but I have lived through trauma, which means I can share with you my insights into what has

> aided my recovery. My trauma recovery is ongoing, and five years into this journey, I am convinced there are no quick fixes for healing trauma. I tell you about a couple of types of therapy, which have helped me recover from PTSD and explore more about how practising relaxation can absolutely contribute to your recovery and lifelong wellness.

Healing is a process, rather than a one-size-fits-all cure. Living in the Western world, I think people have been conditioned to want quick answers to cure their ills. I know I was looking for some way to unpick and rationalise what was happening to me. Life teaches us that if we think sensibly and rationally, then we will be untouchable to the mythological emotional Hydra, which lies in wait in the recesses of our psyche. I wanted to think, '*Yep! Trauma Fixed!*' I was eager to put a tick next to it on the invisible to-do list, which took up so much space in my mind. I was diagnosed with PTSD about four weeks after I was attacked in 2016. Four weeks after a traumatic event is a relatively short time frame for a clinician to diagnose PTSD. But traumatic life events, which had happened a long while before I was assaulted, were still causing me severe anxiety, panic and various other PTSD symptoms. I didn't know I was traumatised. I just thought I had become slightly unhinged and I was doing my best to keep these signs under wraps. Keeping trauma hidden is exhausting for the nervous system. So when I rocked up at the Havens centre in the weeks after the attack, the wonderful therapist, who was assigned to me, was in no doubt that having suffered another traumatic event, the pre-existing PTSD, which I had been trying to cope with, was now seriously impacting my everyday life. I am grateful and relieved to say that PTSD no longer impacts my day-to-day experience. Life feels a lot smoother now because along the way of recovery I have learned a few things about trauma and how to make space for it in my life. When we give space to trauma or, if we can, as legendary John Lennon said, '*Let It Be*,' we create the much-needed internal and external conditions for releasing and healing trauma.

I have a suggestion… Before you read any more about trauma and PTSD, I invite you to do something very comforting for yourself, something that will give your nervous system some respite before your left brain tries to process or understand more information. Our left brain laps up reasoning, analysis and problem-solving, which are all very useful, but our left brain is not helpful for awakening relaxation and self-compassion, which are in fact helpful tools for treating trauma. So what would you like to do right now? Before writing any more in this section, I am stopping to drink a herbal tea (chamomile and hemp brewed for 15 minutes), give myself some dark chocolate and let my eyes feast for a while on a photograph of some soft, voluptuous roses. Being sweet toward yourself at regular intervals will build up your regard for yourself and your resilience while moving through trauma.

Here is a medical definition for trauma from the American Psychological Association: 'Trauma is an emotional response to a terrible event like an accident, rape or natural disaster. Immediately after the event, shock and denial are typical. Longer term reactions include unpredictable emotions, flashbacks, strained relationships and even physical symptoms like headaches or nausea.'

Trauma is a force, which can feel like it has a life of its own, bubbling up with seemingly no rhyme or reason. One moment, you might feel OK, the next, overcome with anxiety and cold sweats. You do not need to attempt to understand, rationalise or explain away trauma. In fact, talking about or describing the actual events, which triggered trauma symptoms, may be detrimental because when we describe what happened, we reaffirm our memory or perception of the traumatic event, keeping the event vivid in the brain's memory banks. When I was recovering from PTSD, I was fortunate to find a therapy that didn't involve much talking about the attacks against me, and I will explain more about this technique later. The nervous system gets too stimulated when the brain is asked to cognate harrowing memories again and again. This overstimulation of the SNS can swiftly manifest as spikes in anxiety, sweating, shortness of breath, blurred vision, body pains, digestive dysfunction, fainting episodes, while the body tries to navigate the fight, flight or freeze response to threat. Being asked to remember, think about or describe in words what we survived can trick the traumatised nervous system into acting like the event is happening again. Imagine the body as if it were a pressure cooker that needs heat and pressure to cook tasty things like jam sponges and steamed puddings. When cooking this way, we do not need to let out all the pressure at once, but instead, we turn the dial a little way at a time to let out enough steam to stop the pot and pudding from exploding and doing damage. If a person is asked to describe repeatedly the sexual violence they survived, it may cause the body's metaphorical pressure cooker to explode because way too much steam (trauma) is let out at once.

Talking about a traumatic event, particularly in the immediate aftermath of a violent act like rape, can make us boil over because we have been asked to let out too much, too quickly. On numerous occasions, I had to describe exactly what happened to me to the police after each incident of sexual assault and rape. I must have told the series of events word for word over 10 times to the investigating officers. The officers were trying to help me by getting details so they could catch the perpetrators, but the more I went over the detail again and again, the more I felt I was starting to relive the events themselves. After one afternoon with the police, I had a horribly vivid flashback to the night of the sexual assault. Saying the details repeatedly meant that my brain activity and thoughts were getting looped in one place, re-living the terror of the attack. The police, who handled my sexual assault and rape cases, were mainly considerate and approachable, but the intensity and repetition of questioning the survivor keeps trauma alive and vivid in body and mind. Most of the time, the police do want to help survivors. However, in my humble opinion, the Police Service has a lot to learn about the impact on a survivor when they are asked to tell and retell what happened. The act of rape is a total powerplay by the Patriarchy. Sadly, the methods, which are used by police officers to help survivors, are formed under the Patriarchy's governance of the Police Service. Achieve goal efficiently (get description and information) and think about the impact of the methods later, or not at all. When I was reporting the crimes, it felt as if the police's drive to collect the information, which they needed to catch the bastards, massively outweighed giving me the care needed as the survivor to not be re-traumatised.

Trauma can feel like a juggernaut of physical, mental and emotional symptoms. I know how scary it feels to be swept into a flashback or to have a panic attack stomping toward you. I have experienced many of these trauma indicators and I promise you that, over time, they will diminish. I used to judge myself so hard for feeling like I had no control over the trauma. *Why can't I just get a grip? I need to be back to normal like yesterday!* While it might have been convenient and useful for me to be back to normal in double-quick time, this was not what my body, mind or soul needed. Trauma does not care that you have stuff to do, places to go and people to see. Anxiety, panic and flashbacks will not be boxed up, filed away to come back another time when your life deems it convenient. However, if you would welcome the possibility that you and trauma are going to be partners for a little while, the onset of symptoms seems less frightening and more like a bunch of sensations that are passing through. I was traumatised at the end of a long-term relationship in 2014. It was not a healthy relationship. Years on and a lot of therapy later, I now see that I had been in a relationship with a person with narcissistic personality style. Had the relationship continued then so would my eating disorder have continued, as well as various other manifestations of a very unkind relationship with myself. The end of this relationship, as with many endings, eventually led to a step toward healing and reconnecting with my true self, but initially, the velocity with which I was discarded (because that is what narcissists do) triggered trauma. After the relationship ended, I tried to hide and to self-medicate this trauma for a couple of years with drink, drugs and more cruddy relationships.

Surviving the attack in 2016 brought me to the Havens centre where I promptly received specialist treatment for PTSD at no cost. The angels, who work for the Havens, (managed by Kings College Hospital NHS Foundation Trust in London) are a huge part of my recovery jigsaw that enables me to write to you today. I am eternally grateful for the literally awesome women who received me there on some of my most awful days. I was relieved to be able to put a name to the myriad of symptoms, which had plagued me and which, due to the sexual assault, were becoming increasingly severe and frequent. The trauma of that relationship and its ending, which I had partly attempted to rationalise away and partly denied because I was ashamed that I felt so off the rails, had not simply gone away or been talked out over tons of alcohol and concoctions of MDMA and cocaine, but had lingered, to grow a few more heads on the metaphorical Hydra. If you are not familiar with the tale of the Hydra from ancient Greek mythology, please look it up. It is basically about a terrifying female snake monster, whose hundreds of bloodthirsty heads grow back after they are cut off. I think this monster is a good comparison for how I felt, allowing my old pain to fester, trying to combat it with substance abuse. The pain always came back much worse. The Hydra story is truly epic reading, but do yourself a favour and do not read it before bed!

Not everybody who has experienced sexual violence will develop PTSD, but it is common. Some trauma symptoms go away of their own accord over a month or so, but everybody is different, so it may take a bit longer. Trauma symptoms, like the ones listed earlier in this chapter, which alleviate over a few weeks, are called an Acute Stress Reaction according to MIND, a mental health charity in England and Wales. Trauma symptoms, which continue for over a month, may signal PTSD. PTSD belongs to the category of anxiety disorders as the sense of anxiety or fear is a prevailing symptom of the disorder. The word 'disorder' may seem intimidating. I think this is because we humans have been conditioned to gravitate toward order and logic. Sure, having a life, which is destructive chaos and overly disordered, is not great for us, but nor is a life which is planned out and scheduled with pristine order. What I am illustrating here is that you do not need to be fearful of a disorder given in diagnosis. The biggest part of this word is **order**, *dis* is only a tiny prefix, implying that order was here before and it will be restored once again. The *dis* is only temporary.

The *dis*order (PTSD), which Post-Traumatic Stress might trigger in a person's life, might manifest as these symptoms, explained in the summary below. Acknowledgement to one of the counselling psychologists at the Havens centre for adding their insights to this section, as shown in a different font.

- Vivid flashbacks, when it seems like the traumatic event is happening again in the present, rather than being an event in the recent or long-term past. Flashbacks do not always mean that you literally see images of the trauma event, but perhaps experience sounds, smells and emotions that occurred at the time of the event itself. People, places and situations can trigger flashbacks. For example, I had a very intense sense of fear when I returned to the area of London near to where I was raped. Sounds and smells experienced at the time of the trauma are also triggers. It is important to be able to identify them and to work on processing these so that they are not a constant trigger..

- Body pain, sweating, nausea, trembling, blurred vision, a fuzzy head and having trouble thinking clearly. Concentration and motivation are affected, so clients are often forgetful and struggle with memory recall of the trauma. The body has a way of remembering the trauma.

- Increased alertness, which might involve becoming easily angered, experiencing disturbed sleep, aggression, being nervous and jumpy (to this day I still jump if somebody startles me), trying to cover up/numb this increased alertness with behaviours like substance abuse or self-harm. Nightmares and sleep paralysis are also symptoms of PTSD.

- Avoiding your feelings by trying to keep busy, struggling to recall details about what happened to you, experiencing episodes of feeling emotionally numb, using substances to try to avoid painful feelings. A person may also experience emotional dysregulation. This is where a person struggles to regulate or 'manage' their emotions.

- Increased thoughts of self-harm and suicidal ideation, both of which require support from your GP or local HTT (Home Treatment team) or CMHT (Community Mental Health Team).

- Continual challenging beliefs and feelings such as feeling you can no longer trust anyone or thinking that nowhere is safe. Psychological and emotional safety is just as important as physical safety. PTSD will often exacerbate these feelings of unsafety. People will also find it difficult to maintain relationships and friendships. This impacts on the person's interpersonal connections with others.

  Some people will develop PTS (Post-traumatic stress) and not PTSD. It normally develops within a month of a trauma and the symptoms are not as severe as PTSD. The person may or may not need therapeutic intervention as the symptoms are not as severe and it's the body's natural response to threat.

  Feelings of low self-esteem, low self-worth, negative beliefs about yourself and the world also have an impact. Your thoughts and beliefs about the world are challenged and affirmed or not affirmed after a trauma.

  There are also co-morbidities such as depression, anxiety and eating disorders. If the client has pre-existing mental health difficulties then these may be exacerbated by the recent trauma. Clients may develop Complex-PTSD (CPTSD) if they have had previous traumas that have not been treated.

> In more severe cases, people may develop psychosis, which manifests into hallucinations, delusions and disorganised behaviours. Note that flashbacks are different to hallucinations and delusions as these pertain to images that are not there. However, the two can overlap.

Even though you may experience feelings and behaviours that are unfamiliar to you while you recover, please know that these feelings and behaviours do not mean that you have lost it or there is something wrong with you. The sexual violence was wrong. YOU are not the thing that is wrong. Traits, feelings, symptoms and behaviours, like the ones listed in this chapter, must be viewed and held within the context of your recovery and are fully understandable, given the experience of sexual violence you have survived, along with any unaddressed trauma or upset left over from other traumatic episodes in your life, be they relationship-based, work-based, race and ethnicity-based, gender or sexuality-based or ableism-based. All the symptoms of PTSD/CPTSD are the body and mind's methods of trying to adapt to living with trauma. Please do not blame yourself for any of these symptoms/methods. Compassion is required when healing from both physical and emotional wounds.

So why do trauma symptoms come on so suddenly and seemingly erupt even though we may be trying to control or supress them? For the answer we go back to the ANS, which we explored in Week One. Your nervous system has its own intelligence, which is not influenced by the rational/thinking mind. Stephen W. Porges, author of *The Polyvagal Theory* (in 2011) called this intelligence 'Neuroception'. It is a body-centred intelligence which, having made its own assessment of a situation/perceived threat, sets in motion its own remedy felt as a set of physiological responses. Neuroception functions outside of your brain's conscious control. For example, when the nervous system senses danger it triggers hyperarousal with strength coming into the limbs to fight/escape, the heart rate increasing so blood can be pumped more speedily around the outer edges of the body, or if one's life is threatened there is potential for the hypoarousal state causing dissociation and/or numbness along with the inability to move.

If the body senses a reminder of when it was under attack (such as a sound, aroma or sight), the nervous system applies its instinctual intelligence more quickly than the logical part of your brain, which then intervenes to assess whether you are actually at risk from a genuine threat needing to be reacted to in the PRESENT or whether the information sensed by the ANS is simply a reminder of a PAST event. Neuroception happens fast, triggering the seemingly correct deployment of the SNS's response (fight, flight or freeze).

If you are in PTSD and you experience a reminder of the traumatic event, this chain reaction of increased heart rate and adrenaline release is likely to feel overwhelming and frightening, and may result in a panic attack. I had a lot of panic attacks while I was recovering from PTSD. One occurred when I was reminded of the appearance of one of the people who attacked me. I froze in a matter of nanoseconds, followed by my heart thumping and a fast onset of shallow breathing with light-headedness.

If the fight, flight or freeze response happens when you are reminded of the trauma itself, it is not your fault. This response is beyond your conscious control. However, by making time to practise generating your body's rest and repair response and by cultivating experiences where the body senses it is safe, your ANS can recalibrate more effectively should the trauma be triggered. The SNS and PNS are designed to be in balance and to work efficiently when sensing genuine threat or genuine safety.

Deep rest and relaxation practised regularly can help us bounce back from reacting to perceived/remembered threats on occasions when the SNS may become triggered, but there is no actual threat, helping us ease into a sense of wellbeing and safety. Of course, if you are out and about and feel triggered or have a panic attack or flashback, it may not be feasible to set up a yoga nidrā nest where you are and do a practice! However, you may be able to find a surface to rest your spine against, let out any tears that come, call a trusted friend and take a couple of slow, deep breaths while your PNS catches up, calming your mind and body. I like to keep a smooth pebble in my pocket and I hold it, feeling its cool sensation against my skin while I take a pause and gather myself if I note that panic is starting to set in. It is when you practise relaxation as part of your everyday routine that you will reap the benefits; helping you return to balance if/when trauma symptoms arise.

It is also possible that rather than diagnosing PTSD, a clinician may diagnose CPTSD. CPTSD can emerge and have long-lasting effects on the survivor if they experienced trauma at a very early age or have had long-term or continued exposure to traumatic events. This can be the case for people who have endured the pain of suffering Childhood Sexual Abuse (CSA). If you have had this experience, then like any sexual violence survivor, you deserve the most expert professional help with your recovery. Please take a look at the Resources section of the book for signposting toward recovery services. Symptoms of CPTSD include long-term feelings of distrust toward society, constant feelings of hopelessness, emptiness and/or depression, feeling worthless, believing that nobody can help or understand how you feel and avoiding emotional connection in intimate relationships. If you are experiencing any of these symptoms, please reach out for professional support so that you can reclaim your enjoyment of life.

In the yogic philosophy, it is believed and observed that all living things have three transitory life states, which change many times during a lifetime. These three life states are 'Rajas', a very active fast-paced energy, 'Tamas', an energy, which feels heavy and lethargic, and 'Sattva', which is the more orderly middle state between Rajas and Tamas. Yoga (and its science known as 'Ayurveda') teaches us that our bodies have the innate ability to right themselves from being too heavily set in any one state and are able to return to Sattva, the middle state of balance.

What has ancient yoga wisdom got to do with PTSD? It is the reassurance, which is innate in your being as human creature, that you have the wisdom, strength and courage to turn *dis*order into order. PTSD can swing us into the more intense end of the Rajastic state; feeling stressed, irritable, restless and on other days suck us into an underworld of overly Tamasic states of depression, low energy or even despair. You don't need to be frightened of the Underworld. We need to access, witness and heal these intensely Tamasic and Rajastic states, otherwise the trauma will continue to leave its imprint. Unprocessed, unwitnessed pain and trauma are not what you want coursing through your body and psyche. When you say, "Yes" to healing your trauma, you are weaving magic, the alchemy of turning pain into precious power. Your PNS will work its wonders when you offer it the chance for rest and recovery, along with intervention from professionally trained trauma therapists. Also, by using the self-directed tools in this book you will find your way back to balance, toward the calm state of Sattva. Should you choose to seek help from trained clinicians, who specialise in treating trauma to aid your journey toward Sattva, you may like to try a type of trauma therapy called 'Eye Movement Desensitisation Reprograming' also known as EMDR or another therapy called 'Trauma Focused Cognitive Behaviour Therapy' (CBT), which are part of a full set of treatments called 'Accelerated Resolution Therapy,' as well as an approach called 'Body-Mind Psychotherapy.'

> *'This too shall pass'*
> **– Persian Proverb**

A Note about Stress and the Body

Stress can really screw up the physical body. I know that I am at the effect of stress when I get a bubbly rash eczema on the sides of my fingers, and when I get a mild bit of digestive trouble. Even though my mind might say, *'Oh no, Sarah, you're fine. You're cool,'* I have come to know that when I get those flare ups, stress IS in the background and then it is best that I begin to put more attention on my holistic health, which is so key to a survivor in recovery from sexual violence. Taking care that I keep my stress levels low means that anxiety and other PTSD symptoms are kept very much at bay.

Whether you are experiencing the stress of trauma symptoms or have been facing more generalised yet chronic stress such as overwork, over-commitment, financial concerns, discrimination, too much doing things for other people, not to mention the potential stress due to always being the one to make effort in your relationships, it is within your interest to try to alleviate the impact of stress upon your body. You may not be able to simply walk away from a stressful work situation or from stress within a relationship. However, if you have continual disquiet in your workplace or other relationships, it may be helpful for you to work with a therapist to help you navigate this or generate the courage to walk away from these situations that do not serve your recovery or your health. Yet, you can employ simple methods, such as yoga nidrā, to smooth out some of the familiar stress responses and to help you feel more equipped to be decisive and calmer when stressful scenarios arise.

In his seminal text, *The Relaxation Response*, Dr. Herbert Benson lists some of the conditions which have causation linked with stress. It makes for pretty stark reading because he lists angina, anxiety, depression, asthma, ulcers, high blood pressure, joint pains, digestive issues as some of the conditions, which get spurred on by the body's stress response to an overactive fight or flight response (the arousal of the body's protective response to get us away from perceived danger). Stress can be particularly bad news for women who, due to a society that would have us believe we can have it all with no cost to our holistic health, are often heading for burn out without realising it. Women have been encouraged to power through, disconnecting us from our bodies even more. Over time, women are ignoring symptoms like irregular periods, cramps, body pains, migraines, IBS, infertility, pre-menstrual tension and brain fog, which are all contributed to by chronic stress. Dr. Herbert Benson evidences how relaxation through focused breathing and muscle relaxation can reverse the physical impact of stress. It may be time for you to visit your GP or a doctor/alternative health practitioner whom you trust, if you are experiencing any of the conditions listed above. You do not have to live with these conditions as just something to write off as part of life. Yes, illness does happen – nobody is immune from getting sick but you do deserve to be well.

Finding Time and Space to Heal

Facing and healing the trauma caused by sexual violence can feel frightening and unsettling to the order of our daily lives. For me, it felt like I was dragging up the darkest parts of myself that I had abandoned at an earlier age because I believed the lie that women have to keep it together to keep the wheels of life turning. Women worry that they simply have *no time to fall to pieces*, which ironically can be the experience of what is happening when trauma is healing. This is a genuine and understandable concern for women who have hundreds of responsibilities. The ramifications of this statement continue to anger and astound me: 'Women are half the world's population, yet they do two-thirds of the world's work and earn one-tenth of the world's income.' – Barber Conable (cited Lucy H. Pearce, 38, 2018). In this world of plenty, women are disadvantaged financially and time-poor.

I feel I must be transparent and diligent enough to acknowledge my own privilege of having more availability than many women to actually dedicate chunks of time to self-care as part of recovery. I have the space to take an hour or so each week to attend a trauma therapy appointment. I am self-employed which makes me time-rich, but unfortunately nowhere near financially rich. The trauma therapy I accessed was free on the NHS through The Havens. I have also chosen to be childless. I know my ease around time and availability to attend to trauma is not the case for every woman. We have children to raise, school lunches to pack, homework to oversee, laundry to hang, children to drop to school and clubs, quality family time to try to squeeze in, meetings to chair, projects to manage, money to make, budgeting the money if there is any, relationships to maintain, big or small businesses to run, basic mental health to take care of, chronic health conditions to manage, GP appointments to keep, meals to plan, food shopping to unpack, university reading lists to complete, caring for older or poorly relatives (much more frequently if they live with you), children's fancy dress costumes to source or make, PTA meetings to attend… and on and on; and so on and so forth. The list is endless. For women, who are single parents, I imagine you multiply the demands on this list by at least two. All these tasks expend your energy on things that are not for you or are not directly nourishing for you. All these tasks are real work and real time demands. I hope that one day women will be financially remunerated for ALL the work we do; job work and/or family work.

I appreciate how taking proper time to heal from trauma does not fit in with the already existing demands upon us women. This patriarchal society has conditioned us to think we need to cram SO much into every day, on top of being all things to all people. The position we find ourselves in as survivors means that for the roots of our recovery to take hold, we must override the coding of The System that insists on a quick fix to problems and therefore keeps us speeding on the hamster wheel. Trauma recovery needs commodities, which Western society has deemed uneconomical; time and care.

As inconvenient as it is, you owe yourself the little or large chunks of time for you that will contribute to your long-term recovery. Perhaps, it means making an agreement with your partner that the children do not disturb you for an hour on weekend mornings so you can take a walk or listen to the guided relaxation for this week. If there is no partner, ask a trusted friend to pick up your children from school so you can get to therapy.

Post-Traumatic Growth (PTG)

When I was trying to cope with PTSD symptoms, which arose on a daily basis for a few weeks, I really did feel like I was wading through a ton of metaphorical shit. I was angry that I was now suffering emotionally, physically and mentally because of the actions of other people. However, even during the times when I would cry in a heap on my bedroom floor or sob to my therapist or have to grab on to a wall to relieve the dizziness of flashbacks, somewhere deeply hidden inside me, I knew my suffering would come to good. I had no idea how or why or what the good would look like, but it was like the little voice in my heart begged me to keep on keeping on. Keep going to therapy, keep journaling your worries and thoughts, keep rolling out your yoga mat, keep setting boundaries, keep doing meditation, keep asking for help when you need it because you are growing through this process.

Some days, the voice was faint and weak, other days, it was like that of a she-lion, ready to tell the world that this suffering had changed me, I would never be the same again and this was good. I started to feel more like I believed in something; something good and real, and just ever so slightly out of sight but I could feel it. It was so strange, because I was furious that the Universe had sent me the experience of sexual violence, but on the flipside my progress in recovery was making me walk taller, stronger, trusting that that I wasn't a lost cause and that one day it would be OK. Being attacked and/or abused is so shit. Nobody should have to go through it. I am not happy that it happened to me. However, my recovery has let me experience life with fresh eyes and a fresh heart, and I know my recovery has grown me like a rose unfurling toward to sun. I want this for you too. Believe in your recovery.

There is a group of phenomena, which the school of Positive Psychology calls Post-Traumatic Growth. This set of behaviours was studied and grouped into the term PTG by Richard G. Tedeschi and Lawrence Calhoun in the mid-1990s. PTG is a modern definition of what many ancient texts such as the lessons of Gautama Buddha taught thousands of years ago, that suffering can have a redemptive quality and can change a person's outlook on life for the better. PTG is defined as a 'positive psychological change in the wake of struggling with highly challenging life circumstances' (Tedeschi and Calhoun, cited Choudhury, 2020). This definition brings to mind stories of Holocaust survivors, who cite their horrifying experiences in death camps as profound growth experiences. The story of Dr. Edith Eger is one of these tremendous growth stories and I recommend reading her book entitled, *The Gift*. The best way I can sum up my own growth is as an inner knowing, which moves between a deep inner peace and an inner fire. We can use the pain of our experiences and direct it toward something good for ourselves and others too.

As you progress with your recovery, you may feel like you have gained a greater emotional strength and resilience toward life's challenges. One day, you may be able to accept what happened and hold the resolve that the trauma does not need to negatively impact the rest of your life. When you notice this, celebrate it. There may not be one obvious day when you suddenly shout out,

"Oh, I think I have accepted what happened and I don't want to have to struggle with it for the rest of my days!" It is a subtle change in perception, which is brought about by working with techniques to help heal trauma (including meditation and deep relaxation) overseen by a therapist, that life might actually be OK, that you are coping OK, and even feel grateful to be alive.

PTG goes a stage further. People, who feel that they have experienced PTG, report that they have felt a positive transformation in one or more of the following areas; feeling keen to take on new opportunities, improved personal relationships; a heightened sense of gratitude for all of life; a deeper spiritual connection and increase in emotional strength and resilience. I can identify with a couple of these factors. Perhaps in time, you will too.

Remember that just because good changes can come from the suffering caused by PTSD, there is no speedy remedy and you need to take your time. When I think about my own journey recovering from PTSD, I am reminded of the ancient Mesopotamian myth of Inanna. Inanna had to travel into the underworld to rescue her desperately sad twin sister, Ereshkigal. Inanna had to meet many aspects of her psyche, which previously she had kept locked away in the shadows, on her journey to the underworld. Inanna was called on to go into the depths of her own unconscious to meet the twin part of herself. She descends underground bravely and consciously in efforts to recover her sister. Her journey down into the Earth is not enjoyable, but when she returns Earth-side she has become powerful because she has taken the time to face the challenges of the underworld. The myth of Inanna teaches us that deep inside the darkest parts of ourselves, which may get dredged up while we recover from trauma, our power waits for us to do the work of looking at these shadows and pain. Recovering from trauma is like descending to and ascending from the underworld and is not something you must rush, in search of growth. I strongly believe women become wiser having weathered PTSD. Your recalibration and growth will unfold in their own time.

Please do not feel that having read about PTG you need to throw yourself at this like it's a target to accomplish. There are no prizes. Take recovery very steadily, get help and notice the incremental positive changes that add up to you feeling rooted in your relationship with yourself and eventually blooming into the version of you, who wants to thrive.

> 'The wound is the place where the light enters you'
> **– Rumi, Poet**

Recovery Guidance for this Week

This week's yoga nidrā is intended to encourage your mind and body to feel safety in stillness while you note areas of the body where you may be holding tension.

Acknowledge your Progress:

At the end of this week, note down at least two bits of progress that are relevant to your recovery.

Five Minutes of Self-Care:

Sitting in your space where you feel safe and free from distraction, place your hands, palms down, on your heart and take a couple of slow breaths in and out through your nose. Make a list of four easy things you can do to calm yourself when you feel any onset of trauma symptoms e.g., my pebble-carrying that I mentioned earlier. Set up one item from your list so it is ready if you need it.

chapter 11

WEEK SIX:

IT BELONGS IN THE DARK AGES—RECOVERING FROM THE GRIP OF SHAME

'Shame corrodes the very part of us that believes we are capable of change.'
– Brenē Brown, Author and speaker

> Slowly and deliberately, inhale through your nose. Slowly and deliberately exhale through the nose. Repeat once more. Feel the connection between you and the ground or surface that is safely holding you. Now inhale through your nose and sigh out your breath from your mouth; let noise come out if it wants to.

I wanted to give you that simple breath exercise above to help to down-regulate your nervous system as we move into the exploration of this week's topic, Shame. Shame is certainly one of the more unpleasant, unwelcome emotions and at its height, may trigger feelings of despair. Feelings pass, if we give them space to be seen and accepted for the transient visitors that they are. I am not suggesting that shame will be banished forever after you have finished reading this book, but you will have a solid advantage over shame's tricky ways.

Approach this aspect of your recovery steadily, at your own pace and with extra doses of self-compassion (perhaps you might like to revisit the guided relaxation from Week One once more before continuing with this chapter).

This week's yoga nidrā is intentioned to help you release and transform any sense of shame, which you may be carrying, that is linked to any life event and not only to the sexual violence. I also invite you to consider that working with a therapist, who specialises in trauma recovery, can be an incredible relief while healing from the grip of shame.

Before we progress, I appreciate that you may not be experiencing shame. The fact that you have survived sexual violence does not automatically mean you have become a member of the non-fun, yet massively oversubscribed Shame Club. It's totally possible that you have been through these horrible experiences and have managed to sidestep getting coaxed into the shame cave, and if this is you, this makes my heart so happy. Do not skip this chapter though because you may still find that the words and yoga nidrā resonate with you. Shame is a sneaky creature and does not only manifest in the thoughts we keep on thinking in our conscious mind, but may live as subconscious blockages that manifest as physical symptoms or body traits, which leave people feeling anything from lethargy to unexplained physical pain. Therapist, Anodea Judith wrote a tour de force book, *Eastern Body, Western Mind,* which explores the notion that trapped or hidden emotions, such as shame, impact us holistically. Consider reading this book if you are as fascinated as I am and want to get your geek on about how our bodies literally shoulder our age-old shame and trauma.

As I've progressed with my recovery, I have become utterly convinced that we live in a world which teaches shame. How come? Let's get some historical context around shame. This is a huge topic, which revolves around the impact of the detrimental aspects of most organised religions; ingrained, forced and beaten into cultures through colonialism, racism and Patriarchy.

Patriarchy is an outdated, dangerous method of control, which has given female-identifying humans (AND truthfully most humans) a revoltingly hard time for millennia through suppression and objectification. As if that were not bad enough, Patriarchy is something far more insidious, sinister and widespread. I define Patriarchy as any speech, action, group or institution, which exists to promote hierarchy, separation and oppression with overall oppression on people who are not male. These facets of Patriarchy all live in the paradigm of fear. Any groups or institutions spring to mind for you?

When I lead my Goddess workshops, I teach attendees that the world was not always governed in this fearful way. You see, Patriarchy stems from the conclusion that God is Male, and he both loves us but can also strike us down dead at any moment (how confusing), so he must be feared and served according to the rules/dogma of whatever religion is being followed. In actual fact, the past shows us that no matter what you wish to call God, Higher Power, The Universe, this all-powerful entity was considered Female for eons longer than She has been labelled Male. The Roman Empire began using religion as a way to control people (especially women and any people who had deep connection and reverence for the Earth) and given that their empire stretched far and wide around the planet, this meant that religion was there to control everybody. The Romans used Christianity to boss people around and make us feel guilty for engaging in anything that the Romans claimed this male God did not approve of, such as folks being able to choose which spiritual path was right for them, be it one dedicated to nature or one, which followed the work of the teacher called Jesus and his companion teacher/sexual partner, Mary Magdelene. However, according to the research and writing of the phenomenal authors Rebecca Campbell and Lisa Lister, tribes were worshipping a Female God as far back as 35,000 years ago. This worship is depicted in prehistoric cave paintings that detail nature, the turning wheel of the seasons and people engaged in body worship. We are taught in school that anything prehistoric is unsophisticated and that people were just bumbling around in a cave-dwelling existence, yet our ancient ancestors lived in devoted cycles with Mother Earth and held nature in great reverence.

Pre-Bronze Age, the earth was populated by many egalitarian, peace-loving, women-worshipping communities. People had grown up with a deep connection to nature, which is the bounty of Mother Earth. So, they revered women and all of our mysteries like our intuition, psychic sense, our ability to give birth and most crucially, our menstrual cycle. The body was something to be celebrated, considered sacred because of its powers to create life and its inbuilt ability to heal. Men and Women gathered for rituals on High Holy days like Yule in December and Ostara in Spring. The Christian Church later hijacked these festivals as Christmas and Easter for the worship of the Male God. Ostara was a celebration of the power of the Mother Goddess since people believed she not only birthed Planet Earth, but that Planet Earth was in fact the Mother Goddess embodied. All human life came through the union of male and female, and had to physically come through the body of woman. This left our ancient ancestors no time for body shaming, the physical form was too precious because both men and women were powerful vessels for creating life.

Enter Christianity, which was made the central religion for the Roman Empire in 313AD, thanks to Emperor Constantine. The Abrahamic religions, which include Christianity, Islam and Judaism, all worship a male off-planet Godhead, contrasted with ancient Goddess worship, which revered the Earth itself and held its people as sacred. People who desired to stay connected to their Mother Goddess worship and saw themselves as sacred offshoots of hers, were forced to adopt Christianity and its singular all powerful male God. Anybody, who refused, was labelled a Pagan heretic and treated as an outcast. Over time, pagan became a derogatory term used to isolate those who did not believe in the singular God of the Abrahamic religion.

Under male-dominated religion, Goddess worship was considered a heretical, shameful crime against the male God. This fed through into the perception of the Female body, which became a target for ridicule and male ownership, its powers of birth and menstruation cast into the dark under the spectre of shame. Images of people engaging in sexual acts were seen as sinful under the watchful eye of Christian preachers. This concept of sin is another made-up construct influenced by one of the greatest falsehoods ever told; Original Sin. This is the belief that all people are born bad and need to be made good by repenting their sins to God. Enjoyment of the body and Sex became a sin, which disconnected people from the sacred relationship with the body, a relationship held so dear to pre-Christian people. If you were labelled a Sinner, then you were required to feel ashamed. Shame ostracises people from the very things that humans crave the most, acceptance and healthy connection. Shame does not want us to be seen, heard, valued or loved. This ancient construct of shame has stalked society since The Church did its job of separating the Female and Male consciousness from their bodies; objects to be embarrassed by and hidden in the shadows.

After I was raped I felt a creeping sense of shame; shame that I had been raped and shame about my body. My body and I had never been great friends having been through years of an eating disorder together, but I was recovering and beginning to feel better about this body of mine. However, the rape swiftly pulled my newfound shaky stability from under my feet. I had unintentionally abused my body through years of overexercise and restricting food. Now after sexual assault and rape, other people had come along to abuse my body in a much more violent way and I had been unable to stop them. Double shame: shame from being unable to stop the eating disorder for so long, along with shame from being sexually violated. I couldn't see that I was a good person because, in my misguided perception, I had let these things happen to me. I became convinced that being raped made my body invisibly, indelibly stained with the imprint of the attacker – that somehow people could see what had happened to me. I had thoughts that I was marked for life as a victim, that I would not be able to look at my body again, let alone trust anybody else to be physically near me. Shame was talking to me, loud and clear.

In my sessions at the Havens, I was sometimes asked what Shame was saying to me. I love how the therapist insinuated that the voice of Shame was not mine. Separating myself from Shame's repetitive narrative helped me disconnect from its grip. With expert compassion and attention, the psychologist supported me to gently examine whether Shame's words were true. Were Shame's nasty taunts that my body was disgusting, based on any hard evidence? There was none. Was there something neutral (and in time, kinder) that I could tell myself or focus on when the shame narrative started running? I told myself, "I deserve to feel better than this." It took me a while to believe this statement, but after some time, it started to sink in. I would literally write it down a hundred times in my notebook or repeat it mentally if Shame made an appearance. Later in my recovery journey, it was helpful for me to personify Shame, disconnecting it further from me and making its visits feel more manageable. I attributed Shame with the physical form of an out-of-touch, prudish, harmless old school ma'am, complete with a Mary Whitehouse type voice and mind-set. Eventually, Shame felt less like a dark, coercive creature and more of an irritating visitor.

During my trauma therapy sessions, I would recall the image of a friendly, safe place, adding in the image of two people I feel safe with. This image of a genuine place was one in which we declared Shame obsolete, unable to reach me. I still visualise the place I picked as my 'Safe Zone.' I used to visit it as a child. It is called May Hill in the Forest of Dean. I am convinced it belongs to a parallel universe where only tranquillity exists. Rolling green hills dotted with ancient woodland fold out like a pop-up book, revealing a ring of towering dark green pine trees. It smells like winter tinged with fresh rain on grass and tender moss. A single Victorian lamp painted with shiny blue lacquer stood proudly, keeping watch. The place seems to have been lifted straight from the pages of *The Chronicles of Narnia* novels, except it's a real place laced with healing magic.

Recovery Ritual: Sacred Groves of Safety

Visualise the image of your chosen place for a couple of seconds and feel free to build up to a couple of minutes of calm at a time. Bring to mind the place's colours, smells and mood. You can listen to my guided meditation for evoking your Sacred Grove in the *Shadow and Rose* area on my website (www.youreenoughyoga.com).

Historically, shame has been used to disempower and isolate women. Women have been shamed and marginalised for anything from having mental health problems, sex outside wedlock, becoming pregnant before marriage and daring to have the baby, being black or brown, having anything less than a so-called bikini perfect body, being labelled as too thin or too fat, difficulties with periods and the whole menstrual cycle (Drunk Man: '*You look like you're in a bad mood, love, you on your period?*' Me: '*No, I just do not want to listen to your BS,*') trying to have it all and daring to drop the ball because we need a goddamn rest, to being told we are hypochondriacs because we (rightly) badger the doctor about this or that unexplained pain and of course the vile fashion for victim-blaming after sexual violence.

As women, we have been trained to judge ourselves harshly against other women AND men too. Patriarchy has dined out on this for thousands of years by suppressing feminine energy and enforcing the endemic negative judgement of the feminine. Shame is triggered, on top of negative self-judgment, by the opinions of other people as to what is good, bad, right or wrong. Shame is part of an old story, more so of a fallacy, cooked up by the male, political priests, who aggressively slammed feminine energy and the female body into the shadows. They didn't understand us nor our superb feminine magic that includes being cyclic in energy, birthing ourselves anew each month through our menstrual cycle. They felt it was dangerous and unfathomable to the linear hierarchies and order of the newly-formed Judeo-Christian religious structures. And so the world's most damaging smear campaign against women began: *Silence them, cast out their beauty, blood, sensuality and power.* They wanted us to live in shame. Shame is not for you and you do not need to keep it. Shame needs to be very much out of fashion and slung back into the dark ages where it began.

Speaking about my feelings of post-rape shame to the right people, such as therapists and other survivors, has helped with my ongoing healing. Are there such people as the wrong people to talk through shameful feelings with? Yes. Early in your recovery process (or ever in fact!) do not attempt to explore shame with anybody in your life whom you feel is judgemental or emotionally ill-equipped to hold space for your recovery. By holding space, in this instance, I mean sitting in silence with you if that is what you need, listening keenly without interrupting, without analysing, skilfully reflecting back what you have said, and using minimal verbal prompts to elicit information. Early in my recovery, I told somebody that I felt like I would feel dirty forever. They were super kind and well-meaning, and said, '*Don't be so silly,*' in their super kind and well-meaning way. BAM! I was back in the shame cave for having a thought that someone judged me for as silly and I told myself I was a melodramatic loser, but I also immediately judged that person as an insensitive idiot for not understanding!

The thing is, we are not educated in how to neutralise shame. I don't recall ever seeing lessons in emotional intelligence or empathy in school. I think things are slowly changing with relationship education making its way into schools. However, being educated in school to be able to hold space for our own or another being's shame seems a long way off. Even though the people, whom we consider ourselves to be closest with, often want to support us and offer various kinds of help, shame can trigger people into being judgemental or overly rational/emotionally frozen because of their own unhealed/unexamined shame. This is not their fault, yet it is neither your responsibility to protect people from your raw feelings. Talking about being sexually violated is nothing to be ashamed of and in an ideal world, all people would be emotionally healthy enough to hold space for these conversations. Unfortunately, we do not live in that world, yet. Begin by letting yourself be choosy about the people with whom you speak about shame, because you do not deserve to be shamed by others about the shame you feel.

You might find working one-to-one with a therapist useful to you and/or a recovery group led by a qualified therapist for survivors of sexual assault and/or rape.

These groups are usually the right conditions for neutralising shame by holding space, offering patience, ideally zero judgement and empathy. Shame needs to be treated not by isolating ourselves within it, but through the right medicine of self-compassion mixed with empathy from others. Silence is dangerous to your recovery. Letting shame stun you into silence only leaves our emotional wounds untended, festering, uncleansed and unloved. Sharing your story with a trauma-informed therapist and surrounding yourself with people capable of empathy is an essential part of your healing. The more we deny, suppress and judge feelings of shame, the more it tightens its grip. My unfashionable school ma'am shame avatar does not need to keep shaming me! Shame does not need to keep shaming you. I promise. The professor, author, speaker and shame researcher, Brené Brown says it so well,

'If you put shame in a petri dish, it needs three ingredients to grow exponentially: secrecy, silence and judgement. If you put the same amount of shame in a petri dish and douse it with empathy, it cannot survive.'

Recovery Guidance for this Week

Time to settle down for your guided deep relaxation followed by Free-Writing. Try to do this practice on at least three days this week.

Acknowledge your Progress:

At the end of this week, note down at least two bits of progress that are relevant to your recovery.

Five Minutes of Self-Care:

Find some roses or other favourite flowers, place them somewhere you can see them clearly as you move around your home.

chapter 12

WEEK SEVEN:

IT IS RIGHT TO BE RAW—RECOVERING YOUR RIGHT TO SACRED RAGE

While recovering from sexual violence we may be met with emotions, which are either unfamiliar to us or far beyond our usual emotional comfort zone. Until I stepped on to my recovery journey I had never been given permission to feel my full range of emotions. As I began to peel myself away from shame's grip, shame gave way to rage. The shame was not mine, but the rage was absolutely mine. Merely, reading the word, rage, may evoke judgements, dryness in the throat or visceral churning in the stomach. I assert that something inside you recognises rage. Perhaps you saw a parent's rage when you were a child and it frightened you? Revulsion for rage may be

> experienced because we are unfamiliar with how to let rage work for us, not against us. Rage is a catalyst for change. Rarely are we shown rage as something sacred, something deserving of veneration or of focused attention, or as something, which forges recovery when we stoke its fire. You are allowed to be enraged at sexual violence having happened to you.

Definition of Sacred:

something that is sacred is believed to be holy and to have a special connection with God.

Definition of Rage:

strong anger that is difficult to control

- Definitions from *Collinsdictionary.com*

We, humans, have a rather skewed relationship to emotions. Unless you were raised by super-enlightened people, we were taught that some emotions are good and some are bad. When people ask me about Yoga, for example, I notice people say they wish they could get rid of their *negative emotions* in favour of positive ones by practising asana or meditation. Getting rid of an emotion is a bypass, which might rob us of the opportunity to be informed or even healed by letting ourselves feel and express these so-called negative emotions. I say it again, the right therapist will create and hold a safe therapeutic space for you to feel and explore the emotions, which we are conditioned to leave hidden in the shadows. Yep, when we leave anger and rage to fester in the shadows and when we do not opt to shine our light on to them, we may turn to destructive behaviours like self-harm or addiction. Accessing my rage with my therapist enabled me to liberate what had been supressed inside me since I was a small child. Rage, safely liberated, is pure strength.

Young children are given praise for behaving obediently and for appearing happy while doing so, because 'happy' is considered as a good/acceptable emotion. *'Oh, you are such a good girl.'* The child is labelled 'good' for showing an emotion, which society deems acceptable. Flip the situation now: the young child appears angry and is judged as behaving badly, when, in fact, the child is testing and/or trying to establish boundaries (which I appreciate for parents may be unbelievably annoying as your child yells 'no' for the hundredth time that morning). This child receives negative feedback from the parent or caregiver because the behaviour and emotion have been judged as negative/unacceptable. *'Behave yourself! Don't be so silly!'* The child and their emotion are labelled as 'silly', thus the emotion (and the child) are invalidated through language. I personally experienced such emotion-shaming as a child in school and have witnessed it more times than I can count as an adult while working with young people, many of whom were suffering neglect or abuse. We may not consciously realise it (with the million other things to get on with while growing up), but we are trained to display certain supposedly acceptable emotions, and suppress those which are labelled as bad or silly. If we really let ourselves *feel* an emotion like anger, or dare I say, rage, we risk so much judgement of these emotions and of our corresponding behaviour that we rarely dare express the truth of how we feel.

Suppressing our emotions may cause physiological stress in the body. Stress means that the PNS cannot do its chilled-out thing, which is designed to guide us into the healing response (see Week One for a reminder). So it is literally in the best interest of our holistic health that we allow ourselves to feel and show emotions like anger, rage, unease, grief, sadness, frustration, despair, outrage and resentment. I was afraid that I would end up like a crazed, wild animal for the rest of my life if I let my rage out. I began to realise that exploring this part of me, bit by bit in a safe therapeutic environment, gave me enough self-compassion to give rage the stage it needed. Indulge me here while I tell you about a favourite Goddess of mine, who embodies the strength within us for which rage can act as a catalyst. Make yourself a warm drink (ginger tea is a fave of mine), curl up with a cosy blanket and let me tell you about Goddess Sekhmet.

Sekhmet is an ancient Egyptian Goddess with the body of a woman and the head of a lion. The Egyptians revered the lion as the fiercest of all hunters in the animal kingdom. This Goddess is one fierce Lion-Queen. Have you ever felt so angry you could roar? Sekhmet was called upon to guide the Egyptians into feeling their sacred rage and invoking the courage to overthrow evil. Sekhmet represents rage, which is justified; holy to that individual and ripe for alchemising into powerful action for goodness and change. Transmuting anger into positive action is a cornerstone in recovering from being assaulted.

Expressing your rage is good for your recovery and good for your relationship with yourself because you are honouring your right to this emotion. Sekhmet does not intend that you hang around in anger forever though, get eaten up by it or feel permanently bitter, twisted and overwhelmed. Sekhmet does not want rage to become hate. She calls on us to give ourselves time and space to feel the rage of what made our heart scream out. Rage can be triggered by many things, be it racism, sexism, ableism, ecocide or your own experience of sexual violence. Sekhmet wants us to feel the anger, express it so it does not destroy us from the inside, nor destroy those whom we care about, through any of our passive aggressive behaviours; all the time intending that anger will come to good.

I interpret Sekhmet as an incredible force for fierce self-love, having enough love for ourselves to go the distance and feel our feelings, including the ones like anger, which you believe you are too much of a *nice woman* to feel. You might feel scared that the well put together, nice persona will come crashing down if you get angry. Well, my love, it might do. I hope you can feel how much I have your back and believe in your recovery through my words in this chapter. The good that can come from indignation about what has happened to you can fuel your recovery. Nobody in this world owes you anything, trust me I spent ages believing that the world owed me because I had been so wronged by being assaulted, but it is YOU that owes yourself the chance to recover and live well. I'm not talking about turning your frown upside down here or any other patronising remarks that you may have been gaslighted with while trying to call up the courage to express your anger. I'm talking about giving yourself the permission to feel justified in your anger, letting it out with somebody who can hold the space for your pain or even setting a timer to beat up your pillow for 15 minutes a few times a week. Always know that on the other side of feeling the rage is healing because letting out the nauseating heartbreak is good for your body. Better out than in.

I love that there is a Goddess who embodies rage. This helps us to reclaim the feminine superpower of anger, which women have been tricked into supressing when it needs to rise, through false messages that when we show anger we are neurotic, crazy, unstable, destructive and high maintenance. Well guess what? Women who show anger can be destructive in a good way, in a change-making way, calling out injustice when we see it and shaking up the Patriarchal structures, which benefit the few and disempower the voice of so many. Sexual violence is a vehicle for stripping away one's power. Rape is the ultimate attempt to disempower. Not only is the body violated, but it is an attempt to silence the voice of the one who is attacked, an attempt to snuff out one's power, to send it cowering back into the shadows. Notice, I say attempt.

You need not worry that once you let yourself get rageful you will stay that way forever. For me, experiencing rage when in recovery from rape is like an altered state, which is triggered by what has been seen, heard, put up with, fought against, been coerced into, forced upon you and, in some cases, normalised to protect ourselves or someone else. Rage is an altered state directed by my fierce sense of justice and my apoplectic unwillingness to tolerate any injustice shown to me and to any women. Underneath my indignation resides love; a tiny flicker of love for the child version of me, who never asked for any of the abuse to happen. The longer I have spent getting strong through recovery, the more bright and brilliant that love flame burns. You might relate to rage very differently, but I think rage is underpinned by a universal drive to right a wrong. Rage can be the medicine to right and heal what you have been through and eventually, to empower you to lend your voice of love to calling out instances of sexual harassment and violence. Or Not. You don't have to become a campaigner or an activist for others. Being an activist for your own thriving and quality of life is enough.

I still get mega angry that I was raped. Almost four years down the road and Sehkmet-Sarah very occasionally wants to tear pillows into shreds. Sometimes, outwardly, it doesn't even seem like the anger is about the attacks. One time, I felt angry with a florist, who repeatedly delivered flowers to the wrong address instead of to my friend, but underneath was my outrage about the crimes against me. (See more on lightning-quick, earth-shaking emotions in my section on PTSD.)

I have fallen into a mind-trap a couple of times that it's bad form for me to feel pangs of rage because I am a woman who teaches Reiki and Yoga, but that is exactly the kind of unhelpful conditioning about being female, which I have already talked about. I call this mind-trap 'having a spiritual bypass'; fooling yourself that being a spiritual human implies you are meant to be love and light *all the time*. For me, life is not like that. Even though I know my rosy-pink heart has so much love to give, I must allow space for the wounded part of me to cry out that *those were fucked-up things that happened!* It's been a learning curve and with the right therapy and support to heal the trauma, I have learned to feel my anger when it happens (or almost immediately when it happens) and let it move through, instead of staying stuck in Rageville. A good friend often tells me that I don't need to squash it down and remind myself to be angry a week later! You will make progress like this too. You see, suppressing anger for months or years at a time will likely leave a person feeling depleted, embittered, tired, listless, hopeless and passive aggressive as their energy drains away after aiming that silent fury towards another person (for example, an abuse perpetrator or rapist).

I will spell it out again that it is completely normal and right to be angry that you were raped, but staying in that anger on a daily basis will eat you up. Consider your rage to be a powerful catalyst for switching on your self-care and self-love like never before. Rage, when faced, accepted and befriended, ignites the touch paper to fuel your recovery. Rage can shape-shift into an unmessable-with love and respect for your Self. Over time, and at your own pace, you may find yourself less consumed by the rage that you have been harmed by sexual violence, and increasingly occupied by your desire to take care of yourself and thrive. You deserve better than to let yourself stay trapped in angry suffering.

Recovery Ritual: Sekhmet Meditation

Take out a pen and paper and let's go on a journey to hear what guidance Sekhmet has for you. You can listen to this guided meditation in the *Shadow and Rose* area on my website (www.youreenoughyoga.com). You can take this meditation as many times as you need if you feel overwhelmed.

Find yourself a place to sit or lie down where you will not be disturbed. You do not have to close your eyes, but feel free to do so if that is comfortable for you. Make sure your spine is supported by a solid surface. If you have an essential oil, which you enjoy, perhaps place some on your hands, rub them together and inhale a little of the scent.

Clench each hand into a fist and then release. Repeat a few times, noticing the tension releasing. Tense your legs and now let your legs relax, feeling heavy. Tense your arms and now let your arms relax, feeling heavy.

Take a slow and deep inhale through your nose and sigh this breath out through your mouth. Repeat this slow breath once more. Give your breath a chance to settle into its natural pattern. Now, slowly inhale through your nose to the count of four and exhale out of your nose slowly to the count of six. Repeat this breathing pattern a few times to smooth out any shallowness of your breath. Then let your breath return to its normal rhythm.

In your mind's eye, see and experience yourself comfortable in a warm place with the sun on your face. You feel good in this setting and are enjoying the welcome heat on your skin. See a circle of light beaming down to you, circling around your body letting you feel protected. A woman dressed in red walks toward you, she looks like you, wearing opulent robes and wrapped in the scent of jasmine. She places her palm up and you place your palm in front of hers, perhaps your hands make contact. Without speaking aloud, she delivers a message straight into your heart, "It is safe to be with your anger. Your anger is for good, not for destruction." She turns to walk slowly away from you. Before she disappears you feel a message from her once again, but this time it is a question. "What does your anger want you to know?"

Take the next three to five minutes to free write your answer. Do not think hard about this. Just let your pen move.

'Nobody objects if a woman is a good writer or sculptor or geneticist if that same woman is also being a good wife, good mother, good-looking, well-tempered, well-groomed and unaggressive.'
– Leslie M McIntyre

Recovery Guidance for this Week

This week's guided meditation for yoga nidrā is intended to connect you to the Earth to help 'earth' your rage.

Acknowledge your Progress:

At the end of this week, note down at least two bits of progress that are relevant to your recovery.

Five Minutes of Self-Care:

Buy yourself red roses, or some other red flowers. Find an image of a She-Lion and decorate this image if you wish. Take a photo of this image and keep it as your phone screensaver.

chapter 13

WEEK EIGHT:

PROTECTING THE INNER SANCTUM—RECOVERING THE RELATIONSHIPS YOU DESERVE

This week's section of your recovery is about making sure you have people in your life who are worthy of your heart and will support your journey toward thriving. When you are recovering from a trauma you need your whole ecosystem (by that I mean intimate relationships, friends and family) to be aligned for your highest good. Maintaining relationships that are not good for you will compromise your health, wellbeing and ongoing recovery. This week's section of your recovery is about making sure you have people in your life who are worthy of your heart and will support your journey toward thriving. When you are recovering from a trauma you need your whole ecosystem (by that I mean intimate relationships, friends and family) to be aligned for your highest good. Maintaining relationships that are not good for you will compromise your health, wellbeing and ongoing recovery. I make suggestions to help you feel into why you may be tolerating relationships that do not support you to nurture your growth, health, creativity, happiness, autonomy and self-image. I explain why unhealthy relationships are dangerous to your recovery.

Definition of Toxic:

pertaining to, affected with, or caused by a toxin or poison: a **toxic** condition, *acting as or having the effect of a poison;* **poisonous**: *a* **toxic** *drug, causing unpleasant feelings; harmful or malicious. Dictionary.com*

For a long while, I resisted using the word, toxic, as an adjective to describe people and relationships that were not good for me. *Nice woman* conditioning forbade me from naming a person and/or their behaviour, which was having a harmful effect upon me, as toxic. If you do not resonate with the word, 'toxic,' insert the word, 'difficult,' instead. However, if you pause to consider the harm to your wellbeing that these people can do, toxic is a much more fitting term. I have a history of being a people-pleaser and people-pleasers do not name and call out abusers. Women are mainly taught to smokescreen by making nice with people. We are taught to nurture, care for and smile. Being nurturing, caring and smiley are not bad things, but they are not things we need to do for people who are toxic to us. After I was sexually assaulted, the rage in me woke up. It was rage and a searing sense of injustice that propelled me to name and stand for the conviction of the man who attacked me in 2016 and for the conviction of the rapist in 2017. I could no longer stay quiet and *please people*. This was the time to stand up for myself. Genuinely, I had never really stood up for myself before. I either used a parent, friend, colleague or boyfriend to fight my corner because historically I was never one for confrontation. I felt that the men who attacked me, had left poison in my precious being and I had to get it out by calling out their toxic crimes. Perpetrators and abusers rely on their prey staying quiet, so their behaviour stays masked by silence and shadows.

Naming my attackers and standing for justice catapulted me toward the edges of a new phase of my relationship with myself. I had never known this Sarah before. I had not met the me that wanted only the healthiest of relationships. I had always been willing to settle for relationships that I told myself were pretty much OK. But, in these pretty much OK relationships, I was subjected to invalidation, control and gaslighting. It is so tough to leave an abusive relationship because of something called trauma bonding in which we care for the abuser and have at some stage seen them care for us. The bond can keep people stuck in abusive relationships along with the fear of reprisal for leaving. Four years after being attacked, I am still learning to establish and define the kinds of relationships I want, whether it be with my partner, friends, family, spiritual teachers and business associates. Weeding out and detoxing from crappy relationships is part of my maturing and growth catalysed by my recovery. Toxic is the perfect way to describe these people AND their antics because they are literally harmful, poisonous to those on the receiving end of their behaviour and I absolutely hope you are not in the midst of fielding and trying to cope with the behaviours of a toxic person. If you are, my love, you deserve way better and I understand that you may feel stuck. Eventually, I want you to keep, forge and maintain only the healthy relationships because a person who has a truly caring circle is more than likely to recover and be able to cope with life and also move forward and thrive 'than somebody who has demoralising people around.' (*What Is Post-Traumatic Growth?* Madhuleena Roy Chowdhury, 2020)

Toxic and harmful are terms not limited to the physical harm dealt by perpetrators in domestic violence relationships or by friends who act physically aggressively. Toxic and harmful also refer to the psychological and physiological effects of these forms of physical violence, as well as the psychological harm from relationships which do not respect your boundaries or autonomy. To name but a few of the effects of psychological abuse perpetrated in people's closest relationships: leaving you feeling not enough, invalidated, demeaned, trapped, hopeless, trauma-bonded, undervalued, self-doubting, confused, treading on egg shells, unheard and unappreciated. You may know some toxic people. These are people who cause you unpleasant feelings by somehow acting harmfully or maliciously. You might know some of these people well or have known them for a long time. You may find them living with you, in your work place, in your parents' home, your yoga studio, your café where you meet friends, at the school gates where you pick up your children, at the local council office where you enquire about waste collection. You will likely be able to think up some toxic people who are in government, big business, banking, or in charge of major institutions. Take the World Health Organisation, for example that is headed up by a man with links to genocide and terrorism inflicted upon the people of Ethiopia. Other examples are the previous and current Presidents of the USA, who have both been accused of sexual harassment.

If you are a people-pleaser or an empath (or both, like me!), it is likely you have some toxic people in your life.

Why? Not because you deserve it or want them around or consciously chose them as friends or acquaintances. Oh no. Some kind, empathic people, who in therapeutic terms are sometimes termed 'rescuers', subconsciously attract toxic people like a magnet attracts iron filings. Toxic people wish to take advantage of or act out their jealousy upon the kind person. They even keep the company of good-natured people to fluff up their own ego.

When you stick around trying to have a normal friendship or other kind of relationship with one of these difficult people, you may be receiving a subconscious pay-off in being able to look like the *nice* person, who actually gets to keep the moral high ground because perhaps a part of you needs validation for being seen as good and nice. Acting like a saviour/martyr means not having to challenge or confront your own drive to tolerate insidious behaviour. I used to need that validation. You may be a wonderfully, patient, kind, empathic person and the world needs more people like you. A strong desire to help people who display lots of drama and tensions in their life, or to rescue them from their chaotic circumstances is a burning fire of a sign that you may be drawn toward a difficult, unhealthy relationship. Your recovery depends on you ring-fencing yourself away from those who cannot really care about you.

This is a non-exhaustive list of behaviours that toxic/difficult people relentlessly perpetrate in their relationships. *Manipulation, gaslighting, guilt-tripping, shaming you, invalidating you or demeaning you, victim-blaming you for the sexual violence, frequently bringing up the subject of sexual violence* (this is likely to re-traumatise survivors), *isolation, too much interest or control over your finances, coercive control, suggesting you should not wear certain clothes or make-up, any physical violence, breaking your possessions, making threats, love-bombing, withholding communication or affection, projection, rage directed at you, unfair balance of housework, undermining you in front of colleagues, friends or your children; any conduct that leaves you feeling less than/too much of something or doubting your intrinsic, inarguable value for simply existing.* These behaviours often indicate abuse within relationships, be it within intimate partner relationships, friendships, families or work places.

What do you do with these toxic people and relationships that you may have spotted in your life? These people will be detrimental to your recovery and wellbeing. I am going to be very straight with you. AS A PERSON IN THE SACRED JOURNEY OF RECOVERY, YOU CANNOT AFFORD TO HAVE TOXIC PEOPLE IMPACTING YOUR LIFE. Keeping toxic people close to you will make you ill across all the planes of wellbeing; emotionally ill, physically ill, mentally ill, spiritually ill. I have lived this toxic-person cycle and, at the time of writing this book, I am very much in recovery and healing after extricating myself away from an unhealthy friendship. While on the recovery path, there have been a few people, whom I have recognised as toxic to me, with the help of very wise, trusted, healthy friends. Their manipulation left me feeling emotionally and physically exhausted; and with the general sense of helplessness and powerlessness that gets conjured in the presence of toxic people. To extricate myself from these relationships has been so hard, so emotionally, physically, mentally and spiritually painful to me, and such a wrench for the people-pleasing part of me that was left over from my past. That said, ending relationships with toxic people gave me a newly restored energy, whereas previously, my energy was consumed in ruminating about why they behave this way, my trying to appease them and having my schedule invaded by their demands.

For people-pleasers, empaths and rescuers it can feel scary to set a no-contact boundary between you and the toxic person, especially if you are someone who has to co-parent with a toxic person. It can feel frightening and discombobulating to move away from relationships with toxic people and to begin trusting your instinct that perhaps had said a long while ago that these people are no good for you. Establishing no contact with a former friend or colleague is a whole lot easier than with a toxic parent, partner, boss, spouse or co-parent of your children. You may tell yourself: *I'm sure they will change over time. It will get better. They didn't mean it. They have a hard life. It's not as bad as it looks/sounds. They struggle to be empathic. I know underneath it all they do love and respect me. It won't happen again. If I keep being patient it will get better. I need to stick around so I get my promotion. I was pre-menstrual and emotional so I know I wound them up. I need to stay for the children. It's just the way they are. They just like to be in charge of the bank account. I am the main caregiver for the children. I must have deserved it for him/her/them to get so angry. They were only violent once. I feel bad for them, nobody else is helping them. This relationship is a spiritual assignment for me* and so on.

So, on go the things you may tell yourself about why you need to stay passive and tolerant of the difficult people in your life. I have told myself all of these things and it was exhausting to continually make excuses for unacceptable behaviour while I also needed to keep my attention on healing from PTSD, advocating for my essential self-care, setting boundaries, feeling my own real emotions, shedding shame, maintaining recovery from addiction and the eating disorder, enjoying nature and demanding justice for the crimes committed against me. Getting caught up and manipulated into crazy-making by 'crazymakers' (Julia Cameron, 44, 1994) was not what I needed to do. You do not need this either. You deserve better than to be invalidated and demeaned by those people who vamp off the good nature of others.

There will be toxic people who are threatened by your recovery and growth journey. They are ones who cannot stand to see you thrive as they are then at risk of being kicked to the curb by you as you start to honour your wellbeing over their needs. Do not expect these people to applaud your recovery back to being the woman you were before the sexual violence as you continue to strive to be a woman who lives a drama-free, healthy, carefree, boundary-selected, enjoyable life. I love that science and psychotherapy are measuring and researching the impact of healthy and caring relationships upon the development of trauma recoverees. *The Model of Life Crisis and Personal Growth* (Schaefer and Moos, 1992 cited Chowdhury 2020) emphasises the fact that what happens to us is often beyond our control, but who we choose to be with, during times of stress, can make all the difference.

Help from a therapist well versed in the effects of toxic people and Narcissistic Personality Disorder will help to set you and your precious heart free from toxic people. If you are not able/do not want to have therapy, there are many other services for helping you stay sane around any toxic people you need to navigate away from. You may like to look up the work of clinical psychologist Dr. Ramani Durvasula. She has an excellent YouTube channel focused on dealing with and recovering from toxic people. I have also included services for support around domestic abuse at the end of this book.

'After any type of abuse, the survivor needs peace, control and privacy'
– Kaya Gupta, Crisis Negotiator and Complimentary Therapist

Recovery Guidance for this Week

This week's guided relaxation is intended to help you connect with the benevolent guides in your life who enable you to feel sovereign and protected.

Acknowledge your Progress:

At the end of this week, note down at least two bits of progress that are relevant to your recovery.

Five Minutes of Self-Care:

Allow yourself to make a list of people in your life, who you suspect, are toxic people.

If you have not done so during this process, try a couple of Epsom Salt baths this week. If you do not have a bath, you can dissolve the salts in the bottom of a hot shower and let the salty steam cleanse you during your shower.

chapter 14

WEEK NINE:

WITCHING AND WATER—RECOVERING A CONNECTION TO THE WILD

> In this week's chapter, I share with you how nature continues to heal me from the pain, grief and shame of rape. You don't need to do the things I do, but you might just get inspired to find your way back out into the arms of the wild. I believe that we, women are inextricably tethered to the glory of the wild, that we are not just on the Earth but part of the Earth's evolving consciousness. Whether you feel that way or not, I promise you that spending some time outdoors, or bringing the outdoors inside in ways that you choose, will awaken the feminine energy (traditionally called 'Shakti') which you can call on to fuel your ongoing recovery.

SHADOW AND ROSE

When I was a child, I adored going on holiday to Cornwall with my parents. I felt like I knew that piece of England from a time before I was born. Playing on the wide, empty beaches in my pink, frilly swimming costume, being a show-jumping pony over the waves as they rolled on to the shore, waving my plastic bucket and spade trophy above my head. I was in my own heaven. I enjoyed seeing my parents relaxing too while leaving the adult world of work behind. I did not have the words to articulate it at the time, but looking back, it was as if memories of another life, a wilder, more ancient life were whispering to me. I realised young that nature is an extraordinarily powerful healer. Then, I eventually forgot and only remembered when I was much older and a bit wiser.

Every year in Cornwall, I would beg to be allowed to visit the Witchcraft Museum. The answer was always no. This left a six-year-old Sarah boiling with indignation. 'What's so bad about it? It's not fair!' I was a mild-mannered child, the kind that my school reports described as a pleasure to teach. I did not give anybody any trouble, and I remember being thought of as shy. Yet the refusal to visit the Boscastle Museum of Witchcraft made me scream, cry and protest until I felt sick. I needed to be in there. I needed to see it. I needed to remember what was fluttering, twirling wispily at the edge of my memory. One day, I reassured my little self that one day, I would get inside that place.

I think I was 17 or 18 when I crossed the witches' threshold. My stomach lurched with anticipation. My Dad accompanied me into the place. He paid the couple of pounds entrance fee for us both. I remember so vividly he was wearing a navy blue baseball cap, fastidious as he still is about not getting sunburned, and carrying a small backpack, with a couple of Penguin chocolate biscuits inside, slung over his shoulder. That day, he played the incongruous, jeans-wearing, softly spoken, masculine gatekeeper to a defining moment of my passage into womanhood. That's how I now read that crossing over moment, 18 years later and coaxing the memory of it down on to this page. I didn't know it was an initiation at the time. Aged 17, it felt like an adrenaline rush, a victory, to be able to walk through the museum door and see and feel what had been denied me for so long. I felt a quiet kind of power.

The place was cold, a relief because it was a humid, wet summer day outside. It wasn't exactly dark, but there was no sunlight coming in and so it seemed murkier than the daylight beyond the walls. It smelled like dry, burning herbs. I breathed it in deeply, deep down into my insides so hard that my heart caught a whiff too. The ramshackle museum was disorganised and archaic, and I liked it. Old drawings of women and men dancing under a dark new moon, paintings of ceremonies with covens watched over by the searing bright full moon, amulets, trinkets, rabbits' feet for luck, chalices, cauldrons, wands and candles, statues of women, horned gods and goddesses, quartz crystals, symbols, geometry, circles, all for the craft of witching. Wild, wild women suspended in time living their wild, wild lives. These were magic people living within a magic land, but so different from the derogatory images of witches my younger self had seen. Barely to be seen were the formulaic images of faces sprouting warts, no evil, mad women ready to turn you into a goat. Instead, I saw the true, wild nature of old, which meant reverence for one's body and reverence for the Earth. Witches celebrated the earth and knew they were undeniably part of Nature. The life of these people was one of seasonal cycles, moon rhythms, nature religion and devotion to the wild lands that they were so indelibly woven in to.

I felt devastated at the end of those enchanted annual holidays when it came time for Dad to drive us back home. A six-hour drive through the backwoods of North Cornwall, South Devon, North Devon, Somerset, Avon, South Gloucestershire and back into Gloucester. I would cry for most of the journey, loud, hard, face-soaking sobbing from the valleys of Boscastle to the estuary at Saltash, as I was scooped up and packaged into the car, driven away from the wild land, which I knew I belonged to. Saltash to Somerset became the unbearably scenic backdrop for my heartbroken, silent weeping; overcome with the desolation at now being so achingly far away from the pulsating fairy-woodlands, Merlin's caves and

THAT museum. The scar of the M5 from Bristol back to Gloucester felt like a sober travesty after the intoxicatingly ragged wild lands of King Arthur's Cornwall.

The wild had spoken to me at that young age and my soul had tried to listen. But I became busy: school exams, eating disorders, education, university, drama school, dating, working, auditions, drink and drugs, men, anxiety, London, work, break ups, more drink and drugs, more anxiety, career change, making money, another career change, burn out, another break up, going back to an old job, raves (drink and drugs), anorexia, getting better, more drink and drugs, sexual assault, recovery, go back to work, another break up, rape. So many of my life experiences had left me feeling isolated, traumatised and disconnected from the natural wild. Thirty-something-year-old Sarah needed to take care of her inner six-year-old Sarah. I think our soul is our inner childlike self, the voice of whom we unintentionally hush up or totally drown out as we navigate the maze of fast, furious, ready-made, domestic, Patriarchal living. Whether or not you believe in the idea of having soul, admitting to yourself or merely considering that you have an enthusiastic, vulnerable, creative, fearless loving inner six-year-old self, who needs you to nourish them with refreshing, nature-bound excitement, can draw you back out into the world, and might let you get just a little (or a lot) wild.

The more I recovered, the more ravenous I became for the wild. I believe that growing up, our connection to the crucial healing power of nature at best gets side-lined, or at worst, gets completely destroyed by the power with which man has attempted to claim nature. The philosopher, Charles Eisenstein asserts that man has tried to do so much to nature except letting it breathe and exist as a part of us and we as a part of it. We are inextricably linked to nature, our souls desperate for a taste of the wild. In an interview I listened to, I heard Eisenstein state that man has tried to 'control, bulldoze, and domesticate the wild.'

The more I recovered, the more I wanted to fill myself up, gorge myself on nature. Truly, recovering my connection with the wild unleashed a part of myself that I had forgotten. I knew this piece of me once, during those times in Cornwall, jumping waves and spotting fairies in the woodland valleys, which spill out to the sea. Memories began to rise up and I'd be shown images of circles, labyrinths etched, carved and tattooed into the wet wood and stone in long-gone valleys, a deafening waterfall gushing into its freezing plunge pool. I would spot wildflowers growing in everyday pavement cracks that I had no recollection of having seen before. Going for runs turned into going wandering. I would throw on the closest thing I had to a raincoat and yomp off in a downpour to Walthamstow Marshes where my gaze would always be caught by the swooning murmuration of water birds of all kinds, swerving over the wetlands. A few times, I would recall the time when I did not want to walk about alone in London, and now these walkabouts were helping to heal me. I acknowledged my progress.

When I left London and got to know Brighton, it was the element of water that drew me closer. Many a morning, I blearily rolled out of bed on autopilot to get this body of mine to the sea. I would slowly, timidly wade out into the water and taught myself not to move too fast or panic when the chilly waters lapped against my heart. In the warmer weather, it was easier to swim having had the humid air wrap around me on my trot to the beach. The pebbles get foot-burning hot but they are a balm when I dry off and lie down after clumsily exiting the sea. Seriously, there is no graceful way to get out of the sea in Brighton because you traipse out of the water over all the stones under the waves and underfoot. Everybody getting out of the sea walks like they are drunk and doing this in the cold is not easy but that's part of it because it's wild. Sometimes, I have my period when I go swimming, giving part of me back to the ocean. For me, that's the right way to do it.

Down into the Ocean I To to Lose My Mind and Find My Soul

As an adult, I had never been enthusiastic about outdoor swimming, but after the rape, I would dream of open water supporting my crying body, letting me float over friendly waves. Before I had to psych myself up to find the courage to even paddle into the cold ocean, I accidentally (except I do not believe in accidents and/or mere coincidence) walked down one of Hove's wide green avenues and noticed a place that offered flotation therapy. I went in and was shown the flotation tanks which are about the size of a small car. The lid can stay up or down while you lie back on the water inside and literally just float because of the enormous amount of high-grade Epsom salts, which are poured into the tank. You are in control of the experience the whole time because you can change or turn off the lighting, sounds, push the lid up easily or just get out of the tank at any point. Floating was perfect for me. I took to it like a floating duck to water. A while after my first few floats, I read that floating had been recognised as an excellent therapy for those recovering from PTSD. I did not know that when I first tried floating, and I believe I was divinely guided in my dreams to find Flotation Therapy. I absolutely, wholeheartedly recommend it to you as part of your process of recovery. The sea, the walking, the wildflowers, those birds, the carvings and all of nature's elements were keeping me alive. Today, I consciously call on and welcome the air, earth, water, fire and ether into my ongoing recovery.

Most of all though, I remember the museum witches and that sacred visit to the building where my eyes were opened to those wild women, who were healers, psychics, wisdom teachers, herbalists, apothecaries, midwives, doulas, astrologers, oracles all of whom revered nature and let Her speak Her healing powers through them. To be a witch is to work with, protect and love the wild. Witching is letting wild elements be used for good, to know one's own wildness, to let the wild be part of your journey. This wild Earth was here eons before us and has lessons in healing for us all, if only we let Her guide us. If only we could let go of our superiority complex of being human and let ourselves feel the wild. We live in Her environment, not the other way around

Recovery Ritual: Wild Altar

You can get as witchy as you like or not witchy at all, while creating a nature altar for yourself. An altar is a space where you can place objects, images, and scents that symbolise the relationships you have with nature. An altar lives up to its name because they can literally alter behaviour and alter mind-state/heart-state. Noticing or consciously spending a few minutes at your altar can presence you to this moment; taking you out of autopilot or a surging ambush of unhelpful thoughts. You don't need lots of space, just a little shelf somewhere that won't be meddled with by anybody so that this space is fully yours. When I was in infant school, I remember the token nature table display where there would be a few fir cones or oak leaves scattered about and some cotton wool impersonating snow in wintertime. I really liked picking up the objects on the nature table and wished I could add some of my own things to the collection. My nature altar is my very own sacred, wild space indoors. I like to place rose petals, a couple of crystals, a few shells and houseplants on mine. Jot down your responses to these prompt questions below and do not overthink it. If it flows, then write a lot, if not, no sweat. Answers might drop into your mind later on or during this week's yoga nidrā.

What do you appreciate about nature?

Have you travelled somewhere outdoors and have you got something that can represent your time away?

Which (/witch, pardon the pun, I couldn't resist) element do you feel most connected with and why?

Do you ever feel inexplicably called to run outside and find a wild space? If so, what lights you up about this?

What kind of nature activity might you like to try when you feel ready to?

Where did you like to go as a child that you haven't been to for a while?

Use your insights from your writing to begin collecting nature items that you can place in your altar.

When you want to change the items on your altar, place your current items back where you found them and say thank you. This completes the circle of giving and receiving with the Wild. Humans have been very much about taking nature's resources with no reverence, exchange or gratitude. Indigenous cultures around the world know they are part of nature's wild bounty and so as part of their culture they give thanks with ritual. Westerners could do with learning from this beautiful example.

It's All in the Plants

I cannot write about the pairing of wildness, reverence without telling you of my experience with sacred plant medicine. I drank a brew called 'Ayahuasca' in 2017 about three months after I was raped. It was not a snap decision or a frivolity because I had been waiting for that ceremony for two years. I had had a passing conversation with a man about plant medicine a couple of years before. "Yeah, sounds incredible, I want to try it," I said. "It's not really for trying, and it's best to wait," he said. "Don't go looking for it, Sarah, let it find you. It's better that way."

Over two years later, I was at a plant medicine retreat in London on a sweltering summer night, waiting to drink the concoction. The timing of the ceremony was perfect for me and integrating the force of nature that is Ayahuasca into my life after that night has been central to my recovery, and central to my thriving.

In many countries, including in the UK, it is illegal to drink Ayahuasca. It has been lumped into the categories of both dangerous and recreational drugs due to Her intoxicatingly vivid acid-trip style hallucinatory effects. This classification of illegal is an example of the Patriarchy's pattern of at best misunderstanding the wild or at worst, criminalising the wild. Let me be clear, Ayahuasca is not a recreational drug to be used for shits and giggles (and you will very well shit after drinking the brew because of Her purgative effect). No, let me say that this sacred plant brew is healing medicine. She is not for everybody because not everybody is willing to be completely under the spell of a plant concoction that will make you clear your bowels into a bag and vomit for hour upon hour while your brain may generate various images . Not everybody will respect Mother Ayahuasca, I realise now that I did not respect her upon first hearing of Her. I was excited and intrigued but this medicine demands more from the drinker.

I refer to Ayahuasca in the feminine form because to the indigenous people of South America, She is called The Great Mother. She has the power to rebirth a person, the power to reconnect the drinker with their soul. Our physical bodies and our souls often get fractured away from one another in the moment of a traumatic event. My experience of being under the watchful all-encompassing eye of The Great Mother and the experienced Shaman, who guided the ceremony, did nothing less than reconnect me with my soul. That heavy, hot night began with me sweating with the heat and pre-ceremony nerves, waiting to be called inside to speak with the Shaman.

This was to be no ordinary chat. Instead, this was one-to-one time (almost one-to-one because his translator was there too) with the fierce, huge heart that was the man who is keeper of the Ayahuasca, to tell him my intention for the ceremony. The grace and power that beamed off that man was like being in the presence of a humongous, walking love heart.

"I have been lost. I want to find my way back into my heart." I uttered my words to him as tears rolled down my cheeks, quickly soaking my face. I had cried so much in those months since being attacked, but it had been nothing like this. I am a crier, I cry at anything, at happy things, sad things, I always have done, but that hot evening in London my heart truly sobbed out its aching grief. Everything my heart had hung on to for fear of speaking out was coming out in convulsing, loud sobs. Everything I had shoved into a grief-stricken pit in my belly, broke an invisible breakwater and came pouring out of my eyes. All the times I had believed I was too much or not enough or unimportant or undeserving, or stupid or weak or dirty or damaged or victimised by being raped. It all boiled up and laced my hot tears. All the times I thought I had to prove myself, be successful, be productive, be silent, let my body be used in a way I did not consent to, or be some other way than I actually am in order to win validation, all those hurts came coursing through me in the majesty of that moment of pure acceptance from a couple of strangers, who would be giving me a supposedly poisonous concoction to drink. The plants were working their magic and I hadn't even had so much as a sniff of Ayahuasca yet.

Looking back, it's as if in that room where I said my intention, all the pieces of a puzzle were being drawn back together over distance, space and time. The child, who believed in magic and witchcraft, was seen and heard, and she would get what she wanted all that time ago standing in that cold, dank museum. I had wanted to feel what it was like to be so close to the wild, to drink it in and feel its splendour. That night I would get what I had needed and wanted for so long. My crying felt so raw and right and the Shaman and his beautiful girlfriend translator just held me in their gaze with soft, unabashed love. For the first time in years I felt truly known and truly safe. They told me, "If you trust the plants, then it's yours."

The Ayahuasca brew is made with leaves from the Psychotria Viridus plant boiled together with the Banisteriopsis Caapi vine. Each plant has a strong effect on its own but when brewed together they create a psychedelic effect on the drinker. The brew contains a chemical called DMT, which exists naturally in the human brain and in many plants. Our gut enzymes would usually deactivate DMT but the vine present in the Ayahuasca brew stops the usual digestive functions and so the chemical is absorbed into the body and travels through the drinker's blood-brain barrier. Tasting the brew for the first time, I struggled not to spit it all out as a reflex reaction. My body heaved and jolted to expel the putrid, foul flavour from my mouth, but the Shaman had warned me of this initial reaction and to be like a warrior in the face of the challenge by calmly swallowing it down. He told me to face a wall, hold on with my hands and slowly walk on the spot so that the medicine could snake its way around my body searching out the places that needed healing. I managed to stay standing and walk a few laboured, slow-motion steps before folding myself down to my mat like a ragdoll as the brew coaxed me into my journey. She had found me and resistance was futile.

I had heard of the types of vision that people have while using plant medicines and the descriptions of ones conjured by Ayahuasca were reminiscent of the sequence in Dumbo when the animals get drunk and monstrous pink elephants parade around the circus. Instead, throw in Amazon creatures like snakes, jaguars and human-sized spiders. Don't believe the hype because everybody's journey with Ayahuasca is different, while perfectly aligned with what you need to see. I didn't see any crazy circus animals but instead I lay on my back and was gathered up in a swoosh of light, which flung me around a luminescent, sequinned galaxy far from our Solar System. The soundscape to my galactic visions were the soft chanting and singing of the people holding the ceremony. The name of the Great Mother was repeated over and over accompanied by the shaking and drumming of percussion instruments. For a while, my purgative vomiting induced by the brew was in time to the chanting. I had a speck of awareness that these were visions that were being conjured in my mind's eye and that I was not actually being twirled around the Orion Nebula, but I was powerless to stop the colours and the lights coming. If you have ever been on a tubular water slide where you get swung up the sides on the stream on water, rounding bends and freefalling down the tunnels, then I suppose my visions could be compared to this, but only very loosely.

My trip was like nothing I have ever experienced in this lifetime or will likely experience again. After about six hours, I felt able to move again, Ayahuasca had me lying supine for hours until now, only moving to lean forward to vomit into the sick bag provided. Each time one bag was filled it was calmly claimed from my grip by the Shaman's assistants and taken away, a new bag left in its place. The purging was utterly gruelling. It felt good and right.

I recall wobbling up to my feet and stepping out of the building into the garden in the very early hours, but what time it was I had no clue. Colours looked different. The trees were the blackest of dark green, as if I could have reached out to touch the leaves and my hand would have been met with wet, viscous paint. The sky was orange and purple and it spoke to me, 'Enjoy the show. It's all for you.' Writing this now my heart tells me that the wild is here for all of us, survivors. It's all for you.

Two important words, intention and integration, must be flagged when one is considering working with plant medicines. Intention is the thing, which you are seeking to heal from, learn and be shown guidance about, and then integrate into the rest of your life. Intention is what the Shaman holds the space for you to get, having listened and talked through each person's reason for approaching the brew. But it is the drinker, who must be willing to show up and fully surrender to the plant, so She may show you what needs to be seen. What you want from an experience is not the same as what you need. Ayahuasca slides Her way into your entire body, mind and spirit to show you what you need.

Integration is being willing to work the plants' teaching into your life so that it informs your daily experience. I have met people who have used other hallucinogens (both plants and synthetic) in a non-ceremonial fashion, with no skilled guidance or instruction and who have not been able to integrate their experience because the setting in which they chose to use the medicine was not focused on healing and there was no respect for the power in the plants or substance from the charlatan running the session.

Plant medicines are a visceral connection for the drinker with the wild, but they must be approached with genuine respect, clear intention and a safe setting provided by experts, along with a willingness to steadily integrate the hallucinatory journey. There are some frauds out there who claim to help people work with plant medicine that do not approach the journey and responsibility with reverence or after care, but rather culturally misappropriate the work of the genuine South American medicine holders. There are also people who sell laboratory made DMT which can be extremely dangerous for consumption. Plant medicine is not to be played with. If you are considering researching and working with the medicine, then think carefully about whether you are ready emotionally. If in doubt, do not do it. Wait, and then wait some more.

No matter how you choose to connect with the Wild, which is inside and outside of you, do things that you feel safe and comfortable with. Getting closer to nature is to allow you to get closer to the true nature of you.

Recovery Guidance for this Week

This week's yoga nidrā practice is intended to bring you closer to Earth's elements and sacred land.

Acknowledge your Progress:

At the end of this week, note down at least two bits of progress that are relevant to your recovery.

Five Minutes of Self-Care:

Brew yourself an edible healing potion! This might be tea made from your favourite edible herbs or a hearty soup or broth made from boiled root vegetables. When you drink it in, feel gratitude and know you are connected with the Earth's energy.

chapter 15

 ────────────────

WEEK TEN:

WOMAN, YOU'RE A WORK OF ART—RECOVERING YOUR CONNECTION WITH YOUR BODY.

Rape and sexual violence really do a number on a woman's appreciation of her body. I had always felt at war with my body and after sexual assault, I felt more inclined to hate on my physical form. For the longest time, women have been bombarded by images of how their body is supposed to look and what it should be capable of. The media must be held responsible for the damage that it has done by feeding women false images of what we are meant to look like to appear acceptable to ourselves and to society at large. Women often find themselves on their

> recovery journey from rape with an already less than enjoyable relationship to or perception of their body.
>
> In this week's chapter, I share with you my work-in-progress journey of improving my perception of my body image and the road to discovering enjoyment of my womanly form. I share with you scientific and esoteric information about how the body is formed into an intricate system, which needs our care and attention so we can remain physically and mentally healthy while we recover, and forever.

I almost did not write this chapter. I tried to convince myself that I wanted the weekly recovery journey to end on the previous chapter. I had it planned out and I felt safe sticking to that plan. I wanted to reassure you that healing is possible as you step out on the path to recovery. I wanted us to delve down deeper into the underworld by spending time on the gorier, shadowy topics like shame and trauma through to the hopeful light back on the surface by encouraging you to spend some time finding out how the wild speaks to you so you can bloody well go and enjoy yourself. I pretended to myself that was it. I thought I would write a book about recovering from rape and smoothly sidestep the very place where sexual violence takes place, leaving the most physical and emotional scars. Rape and sexual violence is an attack upon our sacred bodies; a violation of the very place where you (and your soul) should feel safe. I work in the spirituality and wellness field where much of the discourse on healing (healing from anything) is based on ascending or transcending the body. I fundamentally disagree with this spiritual trope. For women, our wisdom and power is rooted firmly in our bodies and its cycles and so healing must take place which brings us back into our powerful, grounded body centre.

I almost did not write this chapter because when I speak about the body, my body and my ongoing road toward wellness after rape, this is where I have to get more courageous and vulnerable than what it took to write any of the other chapters. This is the part of healing that I still struggle with. Self-doubt told me, *'I must not write this chapter because I am not healed enough, sorted enough or expert enough.'* Self-doubt told me that, '*I am not enough to continue to cheer you on with your courageous journey.*' I didn't mind earlier about not being an expert in trauma, shame studies, mindfulness, human biology or anything else this book has touched on, but my relationship with my body is my Achilles heel. Thoughts concerning my lifelong struggle to accept my body, which have manifested in a history of eating disorders, told me that this chapter would be best told by somebody else in a different book.

Well, fuck that. I don't need to be a certified expert or to be doing a happy dance every day about my body, to qualify me to write this chapter. Despite my ego's concerns about looking like a fraud if I encourage you to begin reconnecting with your body when I am challenged at times to accept my own, and despite the negative self-talk, my heart tells me that there is gold in sharing my vulnerability with you. It is so true that the Heroine's Journey toward thriving after rape is a long journey, mapping its way through twists, turns, and obstacles, but at the centre of it all is our right to live well and with self-compassion for our vulnerability.

In July 2017, I stood on the stage of a busy pub theatre in South London. I was wearing a cement mixer worth of make-up, hot pink lipstick, stockings that rubbed the top of my thighs because they were a bit too tight for the debut solo performance of my burlesque alter ego, Venus Gallactica. I was shit-scared. I also felt more alive than I had in months. All I could hear was pulsating silence even though the theatre was packed and the crowd were going wild. A wave of all consuming calm washed over me before the first long note of Strauss's iconic track, Sunrise (the theme to *2001 A Space Odyssey*) rang out. All eyes were on me. But honestly, that place could have been empty and I wouldn't have cared.

I was performing for myself. It was part of my recovery process because I had been raped four months earlier and sexually assaulted a year before that. I had had a good six months of healing progress under my (suspender) belt after being sexually assaulted at a festival in 2016, so I had signed up for the beginners' burlesque course as an initiation to reconnect with my body, which felt a very damaged and unsafe place. I wanted to learn to enjoy being a woman in my post-assault body while also being proud of my bottom, boobs, thighs and face because as a former anorexic I had never felt good about my appearance. Burlesque seemed a baptism of fire (or sequins!) for my healing.

The rape happened a few weeks into the beginners' course. I stopped going to class for a time so that I could stay home and cry myself through the first round of shock, pain, grief and shame. Being raped was a big, fat set-back, but something told me that I needed to stick with the shimmying and sashaying. I took a break, but honestly I never entertained the idea of quitting the course; Venus wasn't finished.

I am so glad I listened to my intuition. Performing burlesque was one of the most empowering things I have ever experienced because it flew in the face of the rape 'victim' narrative. My first solo gig rocketed by in what felt like seconds, but the effect will last for the rest of my life. Inside, I was still grappling with the symptoms of trauma, regular panic attacks and nauseating anxiety, but I knew I needed to step out for this performance. That night in the sweaty pub-theatre, I felt like a work of art.

Please do not panic, you do not have to start swanning around as a burlesque performer, unless of course you feel inspired to give it a twirl. In that case bloody go for it, Queen! Here's a fun fact though about burlesque; it does not have to involve taking any clothes off. Historically, stripping got added to burlesque a lot later. The original burlesque performed in seventeenth century Italy was about comedy and sometimes satire. I am not suggesting that you need to be doing anything like burlesque with or without clothes. Again, all recoveries are different, but what is the same about all women recovering from sexual violence is that you do not have continue to live disconnected from your body nor from its beauty, its ability to move, its ability to literally support you and its capacity for play, sensuality, good health and pleasure.

Every woman deserves to feel good about the body she lives in. Feeling good, or at the bare minimum OK, about our bodies can be a gargantuan challenge due to the images of the female form that each gender is exposed to while growing up. I used to read all those glossy teenage girl magazines. Back in the late 1990s, I would pour over *Shout* and *Just Seventeen*, mesmerised by the girl models on every page. Pages full of lithe, skinny, tall, willowy, smiling, glossy, preened, perfect and popular-looking, super-attractive, young, white girls. The only thing that I identified with those models on was race. I barely ever saw a woman of colour in those 1990s' magazines.

More than 20 years later, humankind is unpicking and attempting to heal from the impact of the white body being held as the preferred body beautiful by Western mainstream media from print to screen. I did not have any friends, who were not white while I was growing up, and I have no idea what it would have been like to pick up teenage girl magazines and not see yourself represented by any of the bodies on the pages. I can only listen to and be educated by my friends, who are women of colour, about these experiences of not seeing their black or brown bodies on the pages of *Just Seventeen*. Some did not care, but others did. I heard from my friends of colour how they felt marginalised and ridiculed for their bodies while growing up in the UK. As a white woman, I have never had to face marginalisation or lack of representation due to the colour of my body. If you identify as a woman of colour, may I recommend the healing work of Yoga Teacher and Psychologist, Dr. Gail Parker, and particularly her seminal book, *Restorative Yoga for Ethnic and Race-Based Stress and Trauma*. Like yoga nidrā, Restorative Yoga is suitable for everybody, especially if you are new to Yoga. I can only guess at the potential race-based stress that is caused by growing up as a woman of colour in a predominately white culture, seeing no mirroring of your own body in any of the mainstream pop culture. I struggled enough to find a sense of belonging and appreciation for my body while being assaulted with images of extremely skinny models while I was a spotty teenager with puppy fat. Even aged 14, I sensed trying to live up to these images of women was unattainable and unsustainable. However, I was only

14 and impressionable, not able to listen to the wisdom of my highest self, so I felt I must at least try to look like the *Just Seventeen* girls.

I am clear that the body representations of women that I saw in the media contributed enormously to my spiralling into years of eating disorder. The trauma of being sexually assaulted in 2016 was layered on top of the harm done to my body image by anorexia nervosa, exacerbated by years of being bombarded by non-inclusive, unrealistic images of the female form. Women are all shapes, sizes, colour, height and weight, and every form must be represented and celebrated so that feeling included, valued and at home in one's physical form is not an anomaly after years of therapy, but the norm.

No matter the gender identification or race of the sexual violence survivor, the impact of the attacks typically takes a toll on the physical and energetic layers of the body. We all appreciate that we have a body. We perceive it with the senses of sight, touch, taste, smell and hearing. Whether you buy into it or not, the body also has an energetic field consisting of subtle layers of energy. The physical body that we sensually perceive is understood to be the densest layer of energy that makes up the system of the human body. Eastern science and philosophy, which I have been fortunate enough to soak up like a very fascinated sponge during my yoga studies and teaching along with Reiki practice and teaching, use many names for the subtle energy layers of the body. In yogic science

(Ayurveda) and philosophy we have the Chakras (energy centres), Vayus (winds) and Koshas (layers of subtle to dense energy). In Reiki, we have the energy vessels at the abdomen, heart and brain called 'Tanden Points.' Western anatomical science is also beginning to investigate the premise that humans are not only matter, but have a physicality with an electromagnetic field perceived in waves. We also have the inner, subtle body formed of the incredibly sensitive web like structure called Fascia whose layers can hold on to our trauma and physical habits. It astounds me that the ancient Yogis, Yoginis, Rishis, Rishikas, Monks, Nuns, Healers and Martial Artists were scribing their perception of the human, subtle energy body thousands of years ago and, in deeper detail, in texts as early as the fifteenth century *Hatha Yoga Pradipika* (Light on Hatha Yoga).

The impact of sexual violence is felt in all the body's layers and therefore requires recovery in the physical, emotional and energy body as well. Being compassionate and patient with yourself goes a long way to healing the physical and energetic wounds left by violence and abuse. Keep being kind to yourself, your entire body system appreciates it. Let's explore some more about the chakras in the context of recovering from sexual violence, and how paying attention to these energy centres serves to aid your physical and emotional recovery, so that you can continue to live the life you desire and deserve, while continually recovering from the physical and energetic wounds of your experience.

You do not have to be a Yogini, Mystic, Healer, Reiki Initiate or Hippy to have an appreciation for and understanding of the chakra system. Western anatomical science lends itself to unpicking the esoteric concept of chakras, which are part of the ancient Vedic school of thought, originating in India. Chakra means 'wheel' in the Sanskrit language and these energy wheels spin in front of and behind the body. Humans have seven main chakras rising upwards from the perineum area, passing through the central vertical line of the body, up to the crown of your head. From bottom to top, we have the Root Chakra (perineum), Sacral Chakra (sacrum), Solar Plexus Chakra (just above your navel), Heart Chakra (centre of your chest), Throat Chakra (centre of the throat), Third Eye Chakra (between your eyebrows) and Crown Chakra (top of your head).

Each energy wheel, which sits in the energy field in front and behind the physical body, appears at dominant nerve groups that are at tangible points inside the body. Healthy function of these nerve meetings (nerve plexi) ensure that messages can be sent and received to and from the Peripheral Nervous System. The Peripheral Nervous System is like a network of little branches (energy channels), which spread out from the Central Nervous System, which is housed in our spinal column. The Peripheral Nervous System is the keeper of the SNS (fear response) and PNSs (relaxation response). For example, the Root Chakra is correlated with the nerve plexus at the base of the spine, which is called the Sacrococcygeal Nerve Plexus. These nerves produce sensations at the base of the spine and affect health and energy flow in lower anatomy such as the adrenal glands, colon, bladder and kidneys. The base nerve plexus also impacts your ability to feel steady as you sit or stand and affects the health of your skeleton. The Heart Chakra sits before and behind the nerve plexus called the Cardiac or Heart Plexus and needless to say this group of nerves impact the anatomical heart, as well as the energetic heart space of the Heart Chakra, which bridges the lower and upper halves of your body, putting this chakra at the 'heart' of the body. The Throat Chakra is located at the nerve plexus called the Brachial Plexus and the energy of this point governs the health of your vocal chords, larynx and ears along with the function of the thyroid gland. The position of the chakra energy points not only correlates with the physical body's nerve plexi, but also matches your major endocrine glands, for example, the adrenal glands and thyroid. The endocrine system produces hormones that regulate our metabolism, growth, reproductive and sexual functions, sleep and moods. Phew, that is a lot of scientific and esoteric information! Why not take a break for a cup of tea if you feel you would like to?

The marriage of Eastern science and philosophy with our understanding of Western anatomical science gives us a clue as to how both the physical body and energetic field are altered by a physical invasion such as sexual violence. When we add to this, the impact that each chakra is said to have on our emotional wellbeing, it is easy to compute why emotions at best seem a tad off-key, or even totally out of control during your recovery process. You see, the body is not only the place that gets physically injured when under attack, but the body is also the harbour of unseen emotional wounds too. You may only become aware of these lingering emotional wounds when you are feeling particularly sad, frightened or angry.

This is a very brief summary of each chakra's emotional landscape as well as the colour palette noted in esoteric beliefs, taking into account modern chakra theory. It is important to note that the chakra colours and emotional connotations are a relatively new Western addition mapped on to the original Eastern teachings on the chakras"

- **Root Chakra:** A deep shade of red. It creates feelings of grounded safety, ease, and being able to live our sense of safety by having a stable home, having a healthy relationship with money and the will to give ourselves nourishment like healthy foods and rest. These things literally keep us rooted and safe. This chakra can impact our feelings of belonging and trust. And if energy is not flowing easily at the root, you may feel unsafe, disconnected, struggle to 'put down roots' and feel untethered from the ground.

- **Sacral Chakra**: Vibrant orange in colour. A healthy Sacral Chakra is linked with the ability to be creative and enjoy pleasure. This is an incredibly feminine energy centre and, if you choose to, connecting with this chakra can be a guiding light for your whole life and exploration of yourself as a feminine being. It is linked to our awareness of ourselves as sensual, sexual and playful beings, who deserve to have a good time and enjoy the little or big luxuries in life. If this chakra is undernourished, it is very difficult to feel like we have the inspiration to be creative or playful. If energy around this chakra is misaligned or jolted out of place, one may have no desire to enjoy themselves or one feels unable to enjoy activities that they once found pleasure in. This chakra shares its name with its nerve plexus.

- **Solar Plexus Chakra:** Yellowy gold. This is your 'get up and go' energy centre. A healthy Solar Plexus Chakra lets us manifest our desires, goals and carry out actions to create the kinds of life we want. If we are not happy with something, this chakra's energy is useful in helping us elicit change instead of just ruminating, or being in analysis paralysis before making change. Balanced Solar Plexus energy can elicit confidence in ourselves and when acting on our plans. An overactive Solar Plexus Chakra can crank up confidence to a rather unhealthy anti-social level!

- **Heart Chakra:** Did you guess this one? This luscious green chakra is associated with feelings of compassion for ourselves and for others. Free flow of energy around the heart chakra is believed to enable us to give affection and care, and to be open to easily receive it, allowing us be emotionally nourished instead of emotionally drained.

- **Throat Chakra:** Ever felt unable to say your piece in an argument or make a suggestion during a meeting? Unsurprisingly, this beautiful blue chakra resides over our ability to speak out and have our voice be heard because it is so close in proximity to the energy of the vocal chords. An underactive Throat Chakra can leave one feeling unable to speak up for themselves, argue their point or state their preferences when asked for input or decision-making. When I treat female clients at my Reiki Practice, I often sense and feel an underactive Throat Chakra. This is not surprising given that historically and ancestrally our female lineages have been silenced and suppressed.

- **Third Eye Chakra:** Bit of a strange name for this one, huh? Violet in colour, this chakra, located between the eyebrows, is said to be the seat of the strongest psychic power. I do love the idea of having an invisible eye to see what is kept invisible from our human eye. This psychic centre can often give us a heads up when what is being shown to us is not the truth. I feel it is important to note that many women feel their strongest psychic centres are lower down the body, closer to the Sacral and Root Chakras. That's why we have these phrases, 'I could feel it in my waters,' 'I need to trust my gut feeling' and 'I can't stomach that person/place/thing/idea/institution.' The Third Eye Chakra is located at the Hypothalamus-Pituitary Plexus.

- **Crown Chakra:** At the very top of our heads, the Crown Chakra glows with white light and is associated with an individual's connection to their highest self, their ability to receive or download spiritual guidance or, in more plain terms, find solutions that seem to just get dropped into your awareness for problems that have been bugging you for a while. An underactive Crown Chakra may leave one feeling foggy headed, while an overactive Crown Chakra can cause a person to feel 'ungrounded' in the three-dimensional world and too attached to the spiritual realm (think about that person who is love and light ALL the time). The Crown Chakra corresponds with the Cerebral Cortex-Pineal Plexus.

Some of the information above was sourced from *The Key Muscles of Yoga* by Ray Long and Chris Macafort and from https://www.westernwellness.com.au/blog/2014/11/the-chakras-a-brief-overview.html

The chakras' connection with emotions and our ability to live life in flow may not resonate for everybody. However, there is nothing to lose by pondering these potential insights as to where we may need to give ourselves some extra nourishment physically and energetically while we are recovering, and then see if we feel a little better. For example, if you have been feeling unable to make yourself heard or have been putting off speaking out about an important matter, consider giving some attention to your Throat Chakra by taking two minutes to visualise soft blue light swirling in front and behind your throat, while you sip your favourite tea. Or try a herbal tea blended for throat relief – a health food shop will probably have one. If you have been lacking confidence to move forward with a project or act on something that will improve your life, try wearing something yellow for a burst of uplifting colour energy. If you have some time, try the meditation for balancing the Solar Plexus Chakra in the *Shadow and Rose* area on my website (www.youreenoughyoga.com).

Let me connect the dots, if you have not already, between the whole work of art that you are, your body, your health, your emotions, the chakras and the journey toward thriving. Sexual violence can disrupt the main energy terminals of the body both physically and on the level of the energy field. The physical body and its energy field cannot be separated in the sense that we have always addressed them as – as totally disparate entities – even through to the opinion that there is no energy field. That's cool if you are in that camp. In that case, simply think about these chakras as the literal nerve plexi mentioned above. Your body is an entire system. Sexual violence is an attack on the whole system whether you have considered it to be so or whether your therapist/doctor/friends have considered it to be so. Relating to the body as a holistic system can be a valuable pathway for your recovery. Ever heard anybody refer to themselves as a nervous wreck? This is another of those phrases that show how our bodies demonstrate our emotional state but also yield the remedy to these states.

When the body suffers a physical or emotional shock, or has to process the fallout of a traumatic event like a bereavement, divorce, loss of job, infidelity, an illness and, of course, the physiological trauma of sexual violence, then the flow of energy and information (oxygen, blood, carbon dioxide, nerve signals, waste products, spinal fluid) around the body is likely to become disrupted because of that keen bean SNS reliably springing into action to protect us from real or perceived danger. If your body and emotions are busy continuously recalibrating from the lingering trauma and from the upset of being attacked (which is no bad thing, because process, you must), it is possible that other aspects of our holistic system will deteriorate or feel depleted of energy (otherwise known as Life Force in Eastern teaching).

The body might end up sending its Life Force energy into the organs and glands, which drive the fight or flight response, leaving us feeling anxious in the cycle of perceived threat-action-recover-repeat. Remember that these chakras are correlated with the body's set of big nerve plexi and around these nerve plexi are organs and glands of the endocrine system that impact our digestive, reproductive, cardiovascular, musculoskeletal, mental and hormonal health. If the flow of Life Force/energy/blood etc is disrupted from getting to where it needs to go, female survivors of rape may experience digestive malfunction, interruption or more discomfort during the menstrual cycle. Survivors may struggle to balance when standing, due to the endocrine system being thrown out of whack while the physical body tries to recover from the ordeal of the attack. The body barely ends up with any energy to direct towards general health and wellbeing. I remember in the many weeks after the festival attack in 2016, I felt way less than lack-lustre. I felt like a bag of exhausted shit. It was months before I considered that I might like to enjoy life again, much less enjoy anything like prancing around learning burlesque.

After being raped or attacked, it is so natural and normal not to feel drawn to doing things you would usually enjoy. This can last for a few days, weeks or months. Remember, everybody is different and takes their recovery at a pace that is right for them. You must do the same while your astoundingly intricate work-of-art body system does its best to settle into believing it is no longer at risk of attack or how best to ensure your safety. However, if you happen to still be living with your perpetrator please seek support if this is the case. Perhaps keep in mind that you, as a woman, have an incredibly powerful source of creative, sensual energy, which can be harnessed to support the lifelong recovery of your femininity. This power socket is your own Sacral Chakra. Whether you resonate with the emotional meanings of the chakras or prefer to pay attention to their connection with the anatomy of the physical body, a healthy Sacral Chakra or Sacral Nerve Plexus can help you to entirely rediscover your connection with this powerful energy centre and with the feminine energy housed and flowing through this part of your body. The clue is in the name; the Sacral Chakra is truly sacred.

Vedic teaching explores the Sacral Chakra as the seat of one's creativity, the ability to feel enjoyment of life, self-worth and one's sensitivity to relishing life's pleasures. For women, the Sacral Chakra is home to the powerful cauldron of the womb. Whether you have a womb or not, you have a 'womb space,' which is the domain of the Sacral Chakra. The womb space births life, which means that women are literally designed to be vital creative forces in the world. Feminine spirituality calls women, the Creatrix. Whether or not you have used your womb to carry a child and chosen to literally produce life, this sacred space is the watery and sensitive home of a woman's capacity to *allow* herself to birth her creativity and enjoy pleasure. Women are allowed to feel pleasure and it is good for you. These days, I like to live by the mantra. It is good to feel good.' Pleasure can be gained from various pursuits, whether it be enjoying painting, looking at art, riding a motorbike, running your fingers softly over your skin, stroking a beloved pet, enjoying masturbation or sex. Yep, I said 'masturbation or sex.' However, you would like to feel pleasure, let yourself have it.

There is nothing prescriptive about when you might want to start having sex again while you are recovering. If you feel safe and ready, then you do what you want, when you want and with whom you want and that includes with yourself. My only advice is this: you are a precious work of art and you need to be having sex with people who respect and care for you as a work of art. I know it sounds like a major cliché, but your body really is a temple and temple spaces need to be treated with reverence. Of course, if you never want to have sex again – totally cool.

Your Sacral Nerve Plexus influences the health of the kidneys, your ability to process and expel waste from your body both as solids and fluid (intestinal health and bladder). The Sacral Nerve Plexus is often linked with unexplained lower back pain or pains around the kidneys and the health of sexual organs in women. We cannot overlook that the Sacral Chakra and its organs are under direct attack in rape and sexual violence. This is bound to have an impact on the health of female-identifying survivors. In the two years after sexual assault and rape, I had regular and excruciating pains (otherwise unexplained) in my lower belly and lower back which is, of course, the domain of the Sacral Nerve Plexus. I could not soothe the pain any way I knew how and regular painkillers made no difference. Other health issues arose; I had been unlucky enough to have bladder infections from time to time, but after the rape, they became more frequent, longer lasting and far more painful. Six months after the rape, I was hospitalised with a serious kidney infection, which had begun seven days earlier as a urinary tract infection. The antibiotics did not touch it and so it moved up, festering in my kidney. The physical and emotional trauma of rape festered in my body, all while trying to manage trauma symptoms and behaviours, which I noted in an earlier chapter. I recovered in hospital on stronger intravenous antibiotics and morphine. I lived up to my burlesque name, Venus Gallactica because I was a true space cadet on all that medication!

I am convinced that no hospital doctor in the land would suggest that my Sacral Chakra was injured and needed to recover. I had always been open with health professionals whom I met, sharing that I had survived sexual violence and asking whether there could be a link between the aftermath of the trauma and the myriad of symptoms in my lower body. A male doctor politely scoffed at me. A female doctor was very sympathetic, but of course, preferred to deal in the discussion of curing symptoms rather than piecing together the root cause. I absolutely wanted the pain to stop and so my attention was mainly on recovering from these symptoms and getting out of the hospital, but I remained dissatisfied as to understanding why I was getting ill and so frequently. My intuition knows the answer. The pains began after that night at the music festival in 2016, got worse in late 2017 and four years on, thank goodness, I do not suffer with the wall-climbing, uncomfortable symptoms. The processing of trauma and suffering has enabled my body and mind to heal.

Time since the attacks has passed and I have been committed to my recovery through therapy, EMDR, counselling, peer support, dance, yoga, writing, good nutrition, going to my GP and asking for blood work if I'm concerned about any fatigue or other pains, letting myself receive sensual pleasure (which is not only sex, but enjoyment of flavoursome food, enjoying nature, finding things to laugh about), Reiki and other energy healing modalities. These recognised therapy techniques (some evidence-based and some not), movement and lifestyle choices all support the healing of the feminine energy held at the Sacral Chakra, which is so violated when women are raped. From my own experience, the wellness and alternative health world can be judgemental and attack Western Medicine approaches such as General Practitioners, antibiotics, anti-depressants or taking prescribed pain medication. We cannot ignore the problem of doctors doling out pain medication with little investigation into root cause of pain. However, taking medication is a personal choice. Do not allow anybody to give you a hard time about the choices you make which are helping you to survive.

It does not matter if you do not fully resonate with the chakra stuff, but while you are recovering, please take care of your physical and emotional health by demanding good care and answers from health practitioners including GPs and hospital doctors, should you feel you need to be referred for pains or other symptoms that have manifested or worsened after sexual violence. You do not need to tell the doctor what happened to you; rather they do need to give you good care to alleviate any physical or mental symptoms you are having. If you are having discomfort in any area of the body, please seek medical guidance.

You are a holistic work of art and therefore holistic treatment is required to heal the whole being that you are.

Some Ways to Nourish and Enliven Energy of a Depleted Sacral Chakra:

Art, art and more art: Singing a favourite song is art. Doodling patterns or cartoons is art. Putting make-up on just to roam around your flat is art. A two-line poem is art. Writing down how you feel is art. Painting a shelf and re-potting plants is art. Cleaning up or repairing furniture is art. Painting splodges of acrylic paint on walls or any paper is art. Collaging is art. Baking a cake or making curry is creative art. Moving around to music you enjoy is art. Looking at other people's flowers and gardens is appreciating art. Get my drift? Art does not have to be about creating something perfect and pretty for all to see. Art can be a deeply personal and intuitive healing process that can help us realise we are getting back into the creative flow of life and the Universe, as we create in tandem with the Universe, which created us! You don't need to suddenly cover your home in canvasses and slop paint around, (but please feel free to give that a try, if you like, because it is fun). You don't need pricey materials; just paper, markers, perhaps your children's acrylic paint or some leaves from outdoors. The Sacral Chakra bears creativity but it also needs to be fed creativity. As I said earlier, you do not need to do grand, creative gestures with your body or your art, but please do whatever you feel ready to do! Start small and who knows what art may get created for your own pleasure and enjoyment? For arty inspiration you may like to look at the books *The Artist's Way* by Julian Cameron and *Medicine Woman* by Lucy H Pearce.

Spend some time in water in a way that feels safe for you. Remember this chakra is connected with helping us release waste in the form of fluid. In fact, if you want to know something extra witchy, water is the most healing element for the Sacral Chakra.

Look up the Sacral Chakra-inspired asana practice (physical yoga), which is suitable for any level of yoga experience, in the *Shadow and Rose* area on my website (www.youreenoughyoga.com).

Let yourself enjoy something pleasurable. How about listening to your favourite music, calling a good friend and talking about nothing serious or enjoying your favourite food or chocolate?

It is OK and highly recommended that you allow YOU to have some pleasure while you blossom through your recovery journey. Try not to deny yourself the things you already have in your life that bring you joy and lift your heart and spirit. It is healthy for your body and mental health to give some enjoyment to you. You can choose to feel a little better, moment by moment, similarly to how you chose at the start of this book to be willing to move forward and recover.

You are making beautiful progress through your recovery journey. This may be the final weekly chapter of this book, but we both know that the spiritual practice of your recovery will continue.

'We all have the capacity to create ourselves anew'
– Elayne Kalila Doughty, Spiritual Mentor and Psychotherapist

Recovery Guidance for this Week

This week's yoga nidrā is intended to empower you to connect with the work of art that your body truly is.

Acknowledge your Progress:

At the end of this week, note down at least two bits of progress that are relevant to your recovery.

Make a list of any and all progress you have made since Week One. Write down anything that feels significant to your healing and ongoing recovery. Write down what you have learned about yourself while working with this book.

Now make a list of all the ways you will continue to nourish yourself over the next six weeks.

Let yourself dream now. What do you envision for the rest of your life? Why not create a collage or piece of art (doodles are included) that depicts your dreams.

Go back to your wild altar that you created in the previous chapter. Is there anything you would like to change or add to this special place, something that represents the current season perhaps? What might you add that symbolises you thriving?

chapter 16

FINALLY, THE F-WORD: FORGIVENESS

What does that word stir up for you? What beliefs do you have about forgiveness? Take a few minutes to answer this question, to free write about forgiveness and just see what comes from your pen.

For some of us, forgiveness can be a loaded and confusing concept. It certainly has been for me. Let me lay it down for you with some real talk. I believe that telling someone, who has been through a trauma, that they MUST forgive the person, who inflicted the traumatic event, is patronising and insulting. You do not *have to* do anything. You do not have to forgive and if you do CHOOSE to forgive because forgiving genuinely feels good and right in your body, mind and heart, then do not rush this process. Premature forgiveness of a perpetrator does not honour and respect the victim. If you have spiritual beliefs, which you know by now that I definitely do, still take your time with forgiveness because it has to feel like the right thing; and only you really know when you are ready to choose to forgive. Do not rush into a spiritual bypass of your real feelings and trauma and forgive too quickly because it is deemed a good thing to do. I remember being in a personal development course in 2017 and saying that I forgive the person who attacked me in 2016. This wasn't true and I felt that I should be forgiving because I thought that's what 'good' people do. I also felt coerced into being forgiving by the personal development organisation. However, now, with the passing of time and by carrying out practices like yoga and meditation, I feel like my life has grown and I am very happy these days, so the acts carried out against me have way less emotional charge. I no longer spill over into uncomfortable anger and righteousness if somebody asks me how I feel about it. It is like my life and heart have got bigger. I know I am WILLING to let go of the energy-draining hate I have felt towards the perpetrators. It has taken a long while for me to genuinely, autonomously be willing to step away from hate.

Forgiveness is pointed to in so many spiritual and religious teachings; from the spiritual adage of 'letting go of what does not serve you' so often recited in yoga asana classes to going to confession in Catholicism. Christian religious teachings on forgiveness made me bristle while growing up. I went to Sunday School at a Christian church and the message was forgiveness heavy through tropes like, 'Jesus says to turn the other cheek,' 'Ask God for forgiveness,' and 'Forgive us our sins as we forgive those who sin against us,' in The Lord's Prayer. The idea of turning the other cheek always made my skin crawl because I felt this teaching left people open to receiving repeated abuse. In the Gospel of Matthew, Chapter Five, we read that Jesus is supposed to have said, 'You have heard it said, an eye for an eye, a tooth for a tooth. But I say to you, do not resist the one who is evil. But if anyone slaps you on the right cheek, turn to him the other also.' We have two extremes in this biblical quote, one that promotes retaliation or vengeance contrasted with the words of Jesus, which say to give the attacker your other cheek to slap too. I do not believe in violent revenge, but I also do not believe it is a great plan to openly, willingly give somebody conscious consent to abuse your sacred body. As you can see, the Christian view on forgiveness of violence (openly welcoming violence or abuse against oneself) is one that does not sit easy in my heart. I am even more reluctant to ask forgiveness from a Male God for things which He and the original male proprietors of the Christian Church deemed to be sinful, in an attempt to suppress the mysteries of the glorious feminine.

However, there are some interesting things to consider about forgiveness. Having tried on these ideas, I am willing to vouch for them. Take what fits and leave the rest:

Forgiveness does not mean you condone what happened to you.

Being willing to forgive is enough.

Finding it super hard to forgive is very normal.

Working with a therapist can help to unpick strongly held and acquired beliefs about forgiveness. (An acquired belief is one that you were taught and have not examined to see if this belief is authentic for you.)

Forgiveness can absolutely lift a sense of emotional heaviness.

Nobody gets to pressure you to forgive others.

You are capable of forgiving yourself and you do not need an external entity like God to do this for you.

It can be helpful during your meditation to ask for guidance on forgiveness from the Universe, ancestors, spirit guides or from your highest self.

You will not be punished if you do not want to forgive.

Forgiveness is your choice and yours alone.

Journaling can help to process feelings about forgiveness.

You are still a good person if you cannot forgive.

chapter 17

LOOKING FORWARD

So what happens now? You have moved forward so much since Week One. You really have, whether you realise it or not. It is the tiny victories which matter, that are, in actual fact, not that tiny. It is ring-fencing time for your recovery practices like free writing, yoga nidrā or anything else that you may have tried along the way. It is voting with your feet and distancing yourself from those, whom you had made yourself too available to, in favour of making time for you. It is allowing yourself to cry and no longer judging yourself for crying. It is acknowledging that you were harmed and were the victim of an attack, and also that you are a survivor, who refuses to be continually victimised by what happened. These are examples of autonomy and the blossoming of your personal power. Your power is the light that lives inside the rose of your precious heart.

'Survivors don't have time to ask, "Why me? For survivors, the only relevant question is, "What now?"'
– Dr. Edith Eger, *The* Choice: Embrace the Possible

Your path to recovery, wellness and thriving continues. Always take the time to smell the roses.

All the Love,

Sarah x

chapter 18

RESOURCES FOR RECOVERY

Call your location's Emergency Services if you are in mental health crisis or immediate danger.

Public sector services:

For Trans People https://www.gendergp.com/wp-content/uploads/2016/03/Guide-for-trans-people-affected-by-sexual-violence-1.pdf

MIND Mental Health Support https://www.mind.org.uk/information-support/types-of-mental-health-problems/post-traumatic-stress-disorder-ptsd/treatments-for-ptsd/

NHS Resources https://www.nhs.uk/live-well/sexual-health/help-after-rape-and-sexual-assault/

The Havens, London https://www.thehavens.org.uk/about-us/

Survivors Network, Brighton https://survivorsnetwork.org.uk/

Survivors Trust https://www.thesurvivorstrust.org/sarc

Survivors Gateway https://www.survivorsgateway.london/

RAINN https://www.rainn.org/ US based RAINN have an app for survivors with a support hotline and self-care tips.

https://www.rape-dvservices.org.au/ Rape and Domestic Violence support in Australia

Refuge https://www.refuge.org.uk/ For support for those experiencing Domestic Abuse

Women's Aid https://www.womensaid.org.uk/information-support/what-is-domestic-abuse/

BEAT Eating Disorder Support https://www.beateating-disorders.org.uk/ Recovery support for Eating Disorders

Private services:

Better Help Directory https://www.betterhelp.com

British Association of Counsellors and Psychotherapists https://www.bacp.co.uk/about-therapy/trauma-and-ptsd/

Debra Kilby https://www.debrakilby.com/http:/

Dr Ramani http://doctor-ramani.com/

EMDR https://www.emdrassociation.org.uk

Harley Therapy https://harleytherapy.com/we-can-help-with/post-traumatic-stress-disorder-ptsd

Alissa Vitti https://www.flowliving.com

London Trauma Specialists https://www.londontraumaspecialists.com/

Nightingale Hospital https://www.nightingalehospital.co.uk/post-traumatic-stress-disorder-ptsd/

Therapy Directory https://www.therapy-directory.org.uk/

Sarah Wheeler https://www.youreenoughyoga.com/

chapter 19

 ———————————

BIBLIOGRAPHY

A Brief Overview of the Chakras provided by Westernwellness.com

Boundaries: When to Say Yes, When to Say No, To Take Control of Your Life by Henry Cloud

Boycott Satyananda http://matthewremski.com/wordpress/boycott-satyanandas-literature-and-methods-until-reparations-are-made-for-sexual-abuse/

Code Red by Lisa Lister

Don't You Know Who I am? by Dr. Ramani Durvasula

Eastern Body, Western Mind by Anodea Judith

Empowered Wisdom Yoga Nidrā https://traceeyoga.com/yoga-nidra-trainings

In the Flo by Alisa Vitti

Medicine Woman by Lucy H. Pearce

Practice and All is Coming. Abuse, Cult Dynamics and Healing in Yoga and Beyond by Matthew Remski

Pussy: A Reclamation by Regena Thomashauer

Restorative Yoga for Racial and Ethnic Based Stress and Trauma by Dr. Gail Parker

Rise Sister Rise by Rebecca Campbell

The Artist's Way by Julia Cameron

The Divine Feminine Oracle by Meggan Watterson

The Key Muscles of Yoga by Ray Long and Chris Macafort

The Relaxation Response by Dr. Herbert Benson and Miriam Z. Klipper

What Is Post Traumatic Growth? by Madhuleena Roy Chowdhury

When the Body Says No by Dr. Gabor Mate

Why We Sleep by Matthew Walker

Yoganidrā: An Understanding of the History and Context by Jason Birch and Jacqueline Hargreaves

Yoni Shakti by Uma Dinsmore-Tuli

ABBREVIATIONS

ANS – Autonomic Nervous System

CBT – Cognitive Behaviour Therapy

CPTSD – Complex-PTSD

EMDR – Eye Movement Desensitisation Reprograming

FGM – female genital mutilation

ME – Myalgic Encephalomyelitis

PNS – Parasympathetic Nervous System

PTG – Post-Traumatic Growth

PTS – Post-Traumatic Stress

PTSD – Post-Traumatic Stress Disorder

SNS – Sympathetic Nervous System

ABOUT THE AUTHOR

Sarah Wheeler is an advocate for women recovering from the wounds of Patriarchy. She is a Reiki Teacher, Yoga Teacher, Author, self-confessed hummus addict and founder of *You're Enough Yoga* in Hove, East Sussex. She is in her biggest joy when empowering women to uncover the medicine of deep rest and mindful movement through Yoga and Reiki, revealing the truth of being enough; just as we are.

You can connect more deeply with her work at
www.youreenoughyoga.com

www.ingramcontent.com/pod-product-compliance
Lightning Source LLC
Chambersburg PA
CBHW021431080526
44588CB00009B/499